La

LANGUEDOC-ROUSSILLON and western PROVENCE

a countryside guide
Fourth edition

John and Pat Underwood

SUNFLOWER BOOKS

Fourth edition © 2015
Sunflower Books™
PO Box 36160
London SW7 3WS, UK

ISBN 978-1-85691-475-8

Important note to the reader

We have tried to ensure that the descriptions and maps in this book are error-free at press date. The book will be updated, where necessary, whenever future printings permit. It will be very helpful for us to receive your comments (sent in care of the publishers, please) for the updating of future printings.

We also rely on those who use this book — especially walkers — to take along a good supply of common sense when they explore. Conditions can change fairly rapidly, and *storm damage or bulldozing may make a route unsafe at any time*. If the route is not as we outline it here, and your way ahead is not secure, return to the point of departure. *Never attempt to complete a tour or walk under hazardous conditions!* Please read carefully the Country code on page 8 and the notes on pages 68-71, as well as the introductory comments at the beginning of each tour and walk (regarding road conditions, equipment, grade, distances and time, etc). Explore *safely*, while at the same time respecting the beauty of the countryside.

Cover photograph: La Cité, Carcassonne (Car tours 10 and 11, Walk 28)
Page 1: traditional village sign, still seen in Hérault (Car tour 8)
Above: the theatre at Arles (Car tour 6)

Photographs: John Underwood; cover: Shutterstock
Maps: Sunflower Books, based on the 1:25,000 maps of the French IGN (see pages 6 and 70)
A CIP catalogue record for this book is available from the British Library.
Printed and bound in England: Short Run Press, Exeter

Contents

Young cherry trees planted out south of Murs (Car tour 2), with the Lubéron rising through haze in the background — the perfect harmony between man and nature that is the secret of the Provence countryside.

● Preface

This two-volume *Landscapes of Provence* will plunge you into the most beautiful countryside between the Alps and the Pyrenees. Nature has prepared the canvas for these landscapes over millions of years, but man has added colour, form and texture. The straight bold strokes of lavender, vineyards, planes and poplars streak across plateaus; bridges and aqueducts arc gracefully over rivers; sturdy stone towers with whimsical wrought-iron bell-cages stipple the hilltops.

If the harmony between man and nature is the key to the beauty of this countryside, nowhere is it better conveyed than in the paintings of the Impressionists and Post-Impressionists so intimately associated with the South of France — Cézanne, Van Gogh, Monet. Almost everywhere you travel a masterpiece comes to life — an isolated farmhouse awash in fields of scarlet poppies, the limestone ribs of Ste-Victoire rising above a bib of emerald vineyards, stars burning out in a cobalt blue sky over the lamplit lanes of Arles.

This is a guide to the outdoors, written for those who prize the countryside as highly as a cathedral. We want to take you along the most beautiful roads by car and, when the opportunity presents itself, park, don walking boots, pick up the rucksack and *participate* in this landscape. France caters marvellously for all grades of walkers, but *precise* descriptions of tours and walks for motorists are rare. Most touring guides concentrate on history and architecture, while books for walkers often outline the famous long-distance routes (the Grandes Randonnées). But these 'GR' footpaths are sometimes very demanding and, being linear, are in any case unsuitable for motorists.

Our aim has been to describe **car tours** running from the Italian border to the Pyrenees through *many* (certainly not all!) of the most beautiful landscapes in the south of France. The **walks** focus on our favourite beauty spots and are those we feel offer the greatest sense of satisfaction for the effort involved, taking into account the high temperatures and humidity during much of the year. Most of the routes are circular.

The first volume of *Landscapes of Provence* travels from the Alps to Aix-en-Provence. This book will take you through western Provence and Languedoc-Roussillon to Canigou, sacred mountain of the Pyrenees. Use *Landscapes of the Pyrenees* to carry on to the Atlantic coast!

Bibliography

It must be stressed that this is a *countryside* guide, to be used with standard guides covering the area. We always travel with:

Michelin Red Guide: *always use the latest edition*. Useful for finding accommodation, and the excellent plans are *vital* for navigating in the cities unless you're using a smart phone

Michelin Green Guides: Provence and **Languedoc-Roussillon and Tarn Gorges** (both available in English).

A **good field guide**. We rely on the Blamey/Grey-Wilson guide, *Wild Flowers of he Mediterranean*, now out of print but still available on the web.

Other books of interest

Sunflower's **Walk & Eat around Avignon**, despite duplicating some walks in this book, also details long walks in Avignon, Nîmes and Arles — with city maps and a wealth of information about public transport.

Many **French walking guides** are now available locally. Few tourist offices hand out free walk descriptions these days; they prefer to sell you a book or map. If they *do* offer a free handout, it may well be useless (as we have found to our cost!). Most French publications tend to describe walks *very briefly:* make sure that you can form a mental picture of the walk in advance — the climb, the distance, the terrain. Read carefully what we say on page 69 under 'Waymarking, grading, safety'.

MAPS

At the top of each **car tour** we refer to the appropriate **Michelin maps** ('Local' series; scale 1:150,000). For this book you will need maps 332 (Drôme, Vaucluse), 334 (Alpes-de-Haute-Provence), 339 (Gard, Hérault), 340 (Bouches-du-Rhône, Var; scale 1:175,000) and 344 (Aude, Pyrénées-Orientales).

For **walking** we hope you will find the maps in the book sufficient. But if you plan to do a lot of walking in a given area, *do* buy the relevant **IGN 'Top 25' map**. These 1:25,000 maps, published by the Institut Géographique National (the French 'OS'), are widely available in shops, petrol stations and kiosks locally — or may be purchased from your usual map supplier. For each walk in this book, the corresponding IGN map number is shown.

● Picnicking and eating out

Picnicking possibilities are limitless in Provence — especially if you follow the example of the locals and tour with a collapsible table and chairs (seasonally available at very low cost in many supermarkets). Picnic areas with tables are encountered on some of the tours; these are indicated in the touring notes and on the touring map with the symbol ⏚. All the walks in the book offer superb picnic settings, but on days when you are planning *only* to tour by car it is helpful to have some idea of where you might stop for an alfresco lunch. At the top of each car tour we suggest a few picnic spots, favourites of ours over the years. They are highlighted on the touring map, with a *P* printed in green. Where possible we have chosen places where there is something firm and dry to sit on.

There's no point in making specific suggestions about picnic food, as most French specialities are already well known to readers. But if you get the chance to visit a local **market**, it can be great fun picking up your food there. Towns and villages with markets are indicated in the car touring notes by the symbol ♒; the specific market *days* are listed in the Index.

For rainy days, or when a hot meal is called for, we also recommend on pages 175-181 some favourite **restaurants** (indicated in the touring notes by the symbol ✕). These are places we visit regularly, and we have tried to give you enough details of ambience and their various menus for you to work up an appetite! We also explain *why* we have chosen them: sometimes it will be for the food, otherwise they may just be ideal bases from which to 'watch the world go by'.

Misty morning by the Rhône at Avignon (Car tour 4)

A few of these restaurants are at **hotels** where we've stayed to break the car tours. The only hotels recommended here are those we find really 'special' — whether a five-star establishment like the Château de la Caze in the Gorges du Tarn or the very simple Auberge de la Cascade at Navacelles (where you could wake up to the view shown below).

A country code for walkers and motorists

Bear in mind that all land in the south of France is privately owned, whether by an individual or a district. All waymarked walks and other routes described in this book are permissive, *not* 'rights of way'. Behave responsibly, never forgetting the danger of forest fires.

- **Do not light fires** except at purpose-built barbecues. *Never park your car blocking a fire-fighting track!*
- **Do not frighten animals**. When driving, always stop the car until the livestock have moved off the road.
- **Walk quietly** through all farms, hamlets and villages, **leaving any gates just as you find them**.
- **Protect all wild and cultivated plants.** Don't pick wild flowers or uproot saplings. Obviously crops are someone's livelihood and should not be touched. **Never walk over cultivated land!**
- **Take all your litter away with you**.
- **Stay on the path**. Don't take short cuts on zigzag paths; this damages vegetation and hastens erosion, eventually destroying the main path.

Early morning at Navacelles (Car tour 8, Walk 18)

 Touring

The 12 car tours in this second volume of *Landscapes of Provence* take you west from Aix through Languedoc-Roussillon to the eastern Pyrenees. While a few important centres have been omitted for lack of space, we feel that the two books present a comprehensive overview of the most beautiful landscapes.

The touring notes are brief: they include little history or information readily available in other publications (see Bibliography, page 6). *We concentrate instead on route planning:* each tour has been devised to follow **the most beautiful roads** in the relevant region and to take you to the starting point of some delightful **walks**. (Further information about some of the places visited can be found in the notes for the walks.)

The double-sided fold-out map is designed to give you a quick overview of the touring areas, walks and picnic places *in both volumes*. At the start of each tour we refer to the relevant Michelin touring map(s), which

are so handy to use in conjunction with their *Red Guide*. *Important: Both driver and navigator should look over the* **latest** *Michelin Red Guide* **before** *entering or leaving any large city,* so that you have some idea of where you are heading and landmarks en route. It is *never* as simple as it looks on the touring maps, and *hours* can be wasted twirling in spaghetti loops on ring roads round cities like Aix or Nîmes!

The **touring bases** are, obviously, just *guidelines,* and the tours can be joined at any point en route (the major villages are shown at the top of each tour). Since some of the territory covered is well away from popular tourist areas, we chose bases which offered not only hotels, but *our* essential requirements for making an early-morning start: a petrol station and a mini-market! In many cases, however, we broke the tours to spend a night at a 'special' hotel near a walk — like the simple inn at Navacelles or the Grand Hotel at Le Rozier.

Because this is a *countryside* guide, the tours often bypass the villages en route, however beautiful or historically important. We do, however, use symbols to alert you to the cultural highlights (a **key to the symbols** used is on the touring map).

Some other points to keep in mind: **petrol stations** are often closed on Sundays and holidays in the remote areas covered by some of the tours. **Cyclists** do *not* travel in single file, nor is cycling confined to weekends. But on Sundays some roads will be closed off for cycle races: you will have to take a short *déviation. Déviations,* however, are *not* short when they involve roadworks. Especially in spring, long stretches of road will be closed, and you may have to go up to 50km out of your way! French **arrow signposting** is mystifying until you get used to it. You may note discrepancies in **road numbering**: in a move towards regionalisation, responsibility for most roads was devolved to local authorities a decade ago. Thousands of roads were renumbered, but some work is still ongoing.

Finally, remember that **Sundays and holidays** are a nightmare at the most popular 'sights'; monuments like the Pont du Gard or Les Baux should be avoided at all costs. Our tours have been planned not only to take you via the most beautiful roads, but to reach the three-star attractions before or after the crowds. If you follow our advice, but you *still* encounter crowds, we have to admit: we never tour Provence in July or August.

Tour 1: NATURE TAMED BY INDUSTRY

Aix-en-Provence • Rochers des Mées • Sisteron • St-Etienne-les-Orgues • Montagne de Lure • Banon • Simiane-la-Rotonde • Apt • Roussillon

255km/158mi; about 7h driving; Michelin map 340 to begin, then map 334 and finally map 332
Walks en route: 1, 2; also Walks 35 and 36 in the companion volume (Eastern Provence)
Because this is a very long tour, we use the motorway to start. If you can break the tour into two days, take the D96 from Aix, make a detour to Forcalquier and the Observatoire de Haute-Provence, then rejoin our tour at the Rochers des Mées. Sisteron would be a good place to break the tour. The road to the Signal de Lure is very narrow and winding and becomes vertiginous above tree-line; on Sundays and in high season nervous drivers and passengers may prefer to turn back after Notre-Dame-de-Lure.
Picnic suggestions: The Lure mountain is climbed about halfway through the tour. At the chapel of **Notre-Dame-de-Lure** (⩎; photograph page 14) you will find shaded tables and benches, or you can sit on the chapel steps. At the end of the tour follow Short walk 2 (page 75), to picnic in **Roussillon's ocre quarries** (photographs pages 71 and 77); there is ample shade and plenty of room to get away from other visitors.

T he Durance rises near Briançon, a frothing Alpine stream. By the time it has raged through to the Mediterranean basin, the now-wide river runs sluggishly over its pebbly bed, tamed by the many dams and canals which today control its flow, watering the thirsty soil of Provence and powering many industries. From the weird metallic beauty of the modern industrial landscape rising on the banks of this milky-turquoise river, we move on to a totally different 'industrial' landscape — the ocre quarries of Vaucluse.

Our journey west to the Pyrenees begins at **Aix-en-Provence** (described, with walk suggestions, in *Landscapes of eastern Provence*).

Head north from Aix on the A51 motorway.

You cross the **Canal EDF** (Electricité de France), one of the most important canals fed by the Durance. A sign announces your entry to the **Lubéron**, and the mountain is seen ahead, straddling the horizon. The motorway curves round to head east, with the Durance on the left, but the

The Durance at Sisteron

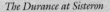

river isn't glimpsed until near **Pont-Mirabeau**, where a picnic area (╥) overlooks the pebbly river bed and desultory streams of turquoise water. The **Durance** is crossed (44km) just west of its confluence with the Verdon (its last major tributary); the small **Barrage de Cadarache** is on the right. Under 3km further on you are welcomed into the **Alpes-de-Haute-Provence**. On the west side of the river wide fields, with enormous gantries for irrigation, fill the space between the honey-coloured village of Ste-Tulle and the spread of Manosque. At the **Aire de Manosque** (▭╥) there are some strange 'sculptures', characteristic of French motorway picnic areas — and a fine view over the wide river bed and frayed stream. One can easily imagine how destructive the river could be before it was harnessed. The motorway crosses the wide Canal EDF again, which in turn crosses the Durance on your right.

Leave the motorway at Exit 19, for FORCALQUIER, ORAISON. Then turn right on the D4B for ORAISON. Cross the spectacular river bed and turn left on the D4 for DABISSE and LES MEES.

The attractive road passes through a flat agricultural plain. Entering **Dabisse** watch for a tiled dovecot on the left. Continue into **Les Mées**: the church, off to the right, has a very attractive wrought-iron bell-cage (♺).

At the roundabout, take the second exit for MALIJAI and SISTERON (still the D4).

You pass the **Rochers des Mées★** on the right (▭╥). Some of these weirdly-eroded

rocks (photograph opposite) rise to 150m/500ft. There is a picnic area, but little shade. The road crosses the impressive **Canal d'Oraison**.

At a roundabout (95km), keep ahead for DIGNE, crossing the Bléone. At the next roundabout take the third exit for SISTERON.

Now you're on the N85 (the '**Route Napoléon**'; Car tour 4 in the *Eastern Provence* volume). You cross the fast-flowing Canal d'Oraison again and then keep it on your right. On the left, in the distance, is the large lump of the Montagne de Lure.

Just before the N85 crosses the Durance, take the D4 for L'ESCALE and VOLONNE, crossing the Canal d'Oraison for a third time. Now refer to map 334.

Beyond **L'Escale** you climb above the Durance — note its stronger flow as you head north. From **Volonne** the D4 climbs to a plateau cultivated with cereals and other crops, below a backdrop of mountains. The remains of the 11th-century Romanesque chapel of **St-Martin** stand off to the right on a hill. You crest a rise and have a fine view of Sisteron ahead. Below is the dam where the canal takes its water.

At a roundabout, take the second exit for SISTERON CENTRE.

Just over 0.5km beyond the **Tunnel de la Baume**, you can pull up left at a viewpoint★ (▭) towards Sisteron, with its 12th/16th-century citadel rising on a sheer buttress of rock (photograph page 11).

Some 0.5km further on, turn left for CENTRE VILLE/GAP, crossing the Durance. Take the

According to legend, the Rocher des Mées (or 'The Penitents') are robed monks, turned to stone by St Donat. Their crime was to lust after beautiful Moorish women captured by a local lord during the Saracen invasions.

second exit at the next round-about, to drive through a tunnel beneath the citadel. *Keep following* CENTRE VILLE.

Park and stroll around **Sisteron**★ (115km *i*✝🏰⛪), a good overnight base. Aside from the citadel, be sure to see the former cathedral (12th-century Notre-Dame-des-Pommiers) and the clock tower with its lovely wrought-iron bell-cage. A key staging-post throughout history, Sisteron was on the Via Domitia link-ing the Alps with the Rhône Delta; almost 1500 years later, Napoléon stopped here for lunch on his triumphal return from exile on Elba.

The next part of the tour visits the Montagne de Lure, which *can* be approached from just outside Sisteron. We do not recommend this route, how-ever: not only is the north side of the mountain less attractive, but the road is often in *very poor* condition, vertiginous, and prone to rock-falls. We head *south* from Sisteron.

Keep ahead on the D4085

towards AIX and DIGNE. After 6.5km, at a roundabout, take the first exit for ST-ETIENNE and PEIPIN (D703).

After passing to the right of **Peipin**, this very pretty country lane (now the D951) is edged on the left by an unusual 'neck-lace' of low grey hillocks, set off by a collar of colourful crops. Beyond the vivid green fields of **Les Paulons** you come to **Châteauneuf**.

The pilgrimage church of St-Donat

Bear right with the D951 for ST-ETIENNE and PEYRUIS. Pass Châteauneuf's church on the left and then turn left for PEYRUIS on the D801, another country lane. After 3.5km, go left on the D101 for PEYRUIS.

Soon the 14th-century pilgrimage church of **St-Donat★** (🛉) is seen on a wooded hillside to the right. This well-restored example of early Romanesque art rises on the site where the hermit saint (whose monks pay penance at Les Mées) retired in the 6th century.

Return to the last junction and fork left on the D101.

Now the Lure mountain is a big green mound ahead, and you pass a massive quarry.

When you meet the D951 again, turn left.

Beyond **Mallefougasse** a wide valley opens up on the left. You squeeze through **Cruis**, a pretty hamlet with a simple church. The beautiful valley road, bordered by fields, takes you to **St-Etienne-les-Orgues** (150km *i* 🏖 and 13/18th-century 🗐), where the lovely village nucleus is off to the left.

After passing to the right of the church with its sharply-pointed spire, go right on the D413 (later D113) to climb the MONTAGNE DE LURE.

Crawl up in hairpin bends through lavender fields and then a forest of mixed conifers. About 10km uphill, not far beyond a shrine on the left, turn right along a potholed track to **Notre-Dame-de-Lure** (161km 🛉🏔; photograph below). This site is also associated with St Donat, who founded a hermitage near here in the 5th century.

Return to the D113 and turn right uphill, passing a refuge on the right and then a hotel and ski-run (which badly disfigure the landscape in summer). At the Y-fork go either way; the roads rejoin. Now, having climbed above tree-line, you can enjoy wonderful views down off the white scree-slopes of the **Montagne de Lure★**, dotted with dwarf junipers. From a pass you look out toward the

Notre-Dame-de-Lure. Ancient trees shade this small chapel, built above the remains of a simple 12th-century monastery. According to legend, there was a hermitage near this site as early as the 5th century.

snow-capped Alps. The road is noticeably vertiginous now; the edge is not built up at the side. Pass the road to the Signal de Lure (1826m/6000ft) and come over another pass — to fine, if hazy, views of Mont Ventoux, the Cévennes, the Alps and the coast.

Turn round here, back to St-Etienne (193km), and continue southwest on the D951.

You pass two tiny chapels on the right, St-Joseph and St-Sebastien. The **Laye Valley** below on the left is a patchwork of colour studded with low stone farm buildings and stands of trees offering shade to flocks of sheep.

At a fork, ignore the D112 right to Ongles; keep left on the D951 for BANON. Just past some faded red and ochre buildings up on the right, turn right for BANON on the D950.

The road runs through rolling hillocks, where emerald cultivation and woodland alternate. Set like a tiny gem on the right is the old honey-hued kernel of **Le Largue**, its tiny church weighed down by two large bells in a wall-belfry. You pass the Romanesque chapel of **Notre-Dame-des-Anges** on a hillock to the right, screened from view by roadside trees. **Banon** (🍴) is renowned for its goats' cheeses wrapped in chestnut leaves, but our abiding memory of this village is the rainbow of shutters.

From Banon centre turn left to the village bypass, then turn right. From the petrol station take the D51 left for SIMIANE.

You cross a plateau. Some fields of lavender paint attractive stripes in the landscape as you approach gorgeous **Simiane-la-Rotonde★** (◻).

Honey-coloured houses spill down the hill from the focal point — the eponymous rotunda, all that remains of the 12th-century château/dungeon of the counts of Simiane.

*The wooded D51 becomes the D22 when you enter **Vaucluse**.*

Soon the **Calavon Valley** opens up on the left — a Swiss-Alpine landscape, with rolling green hills and a lake.

At a fork, turn right with the D22 for RUSTREL and GIGNAC.

The road now follows the **river Dôa**. Soon the ochre quarries of the **Colorado Provençal★** are seen to the left, adding colour and texture to the tapestry of fields. Just metres before the D30a right into Rustrel (🍴), you could turn *left* to explore these old quarries on foot (Walk 1; photograph pages 72-73).

From here the tour makes for Apt and then Roussillon. *But if by chance you are here on a Saturday, don't try to drive through Apt;* take a detour via St-Saturnin to the north. **Apt** (244km *i*🍴⌂), capital of the Lubéron and one of the world's largest producers of candied fruits, springs to life on Saturdays, when the whole town is taken over by a vibrant market.

Leave Apt on the D900 for AVIGNON and CAVAILLON (refer to map 332). After 4.5km turn right on the D4. Then go left on the D104 for ROUSSILLON.

Crimson **Roussillon★** (255km *i*🍴⌂), perched atop gouged-out ochre quarries, is one of the most beautiful villages in Provence and a fine touring base. Walk 2 (photograph page 71) is an easy introduction to this extravaganza of colour, best seen under a low sun.

Tour 2: THE LUBERON

Roussillon • Forêt de Venasque • Abbaye de Sénanque • Gordes • Combe de Vidauque • Abbaye de Silvacane • Cadenet • Forêt des Cèdres • Saignon • Roussillon

166km/103mi; about 6h driving; Michelin map 332
Walks en route: 2, 3, 4, 5
Roads are varied — some narrow and winding, others wide and fairly busy. In places the road from the Forêt de Venasque to the Abbaye de Sénanque is only wide enough for one car, and you may have to back up for touring coaches.
Picnic suggestions: There are delightful settings on the Lubéron, but nothing to sit on.

The **Combe de Vidauque** (early in the tour) offers superb views from a rock garden of wild flowers, but no shade. As you climb to the **Forêt des Cèdres** (over halfway through the tour) you could park 3.3km uphill for superb views over Lacoste and Bonnieux; some shade. There are no views in the cedar forest on the summit, but it is cool and sweet-scented. Also **Roussillon** (see Car tour 1).

The Lubéron, a 60km/37mi-long wooded massif, stretches east to west in the cradle of the Durance between Manosque and Avignon. Seen from a distance, the range betrays nothing of its limestone crags and ravines; it rises gently off the plain in one great mass of emerald greenery. Its shape is unmistakable — reminiscent of a giant cat in slumber. Whatever time of year you climb its flanks, nature will put on a superb display: the lavender fields of Sénanque and the Vaucluse Plateau are best seen in high summer, the Combe de Vidauque in late spring, and the foothills in autumn, when the vineyards weave a tapestry of reds and golds.

*Leave **Roussillon** on the D227 (APT, ST-SATURNIN, MURS). Join the D4 and turn left (MURS, CARPENTRAS).*

The road winds through orchards and vineyards (photograph pages 4-5) but, as you reach the **Plateau de Vaucluse**, *garrigues* take over. Soon **Murs** stretches out ahead (🏛); a delicate wrought-iron bell-cage and the 16th-century castle with bartizans are visible.

Keep straight ahead, to leave Murs on the D4 to VENASQUE.

Under 4km outside Murs there is a superb view left (📷) to the Lubéron, with orchards and farmlands in the foreground. From the **Col de**

Murs continue downhill through the oaks of the **Forêt de Venasque**. Soon you're in a grey-rock gorge, which is dry for most of the year (🍽).

At the next crossroads turn left on the D177 for GORDES, ABBAYE DE SENANQUE (or first continue ahead to Venasque, to see one of the oldest religious buildings in France, the 6th-century Merovingian baptistry; a detour of 8km return).

The D177 follows a more impressive gorge (best seen in autumn for the foliage), but it too is dry for most of the year. After winding down the **Sénancole Valley** through mixed woodlands, you come

Coustellet's very large Sunday morning market is worth a visit if you're in the area

upon the turn-off left, with a superb view (📷) over fields of lavender to the isolated 12th-century Romanesque **Abbaye de Sénanque★** (31.5km 🏃). Walk 3 passes this way; see photograph page 79. Sénanque is one of three important Cistercian abbeys in Provence, a 'sister' to the Abbaye de Silvacane (visited later in the tour) and Le Thoronet (a detour on Car tour 8 in *Landscapes of eastern Provence*).

From the abbey the road to Gordes is very narrow but, if there are no cars or coaches around, you can pull up in a passing bay for more superb views down onto the abbey's setting. At the **Côte de Sénanque** (indicated only on some walkers' signposts, from where the GR6 descends to Gordes), there's an excellent view down over the plain towards the Petit Lubéron (32km 📷; 🚶 0.7km downhill). Now you enter the world of the 'bories' and the beautiful, incredibly intricate drystone walls that surround Gordes (see photograph and notes page 79).

Meeting the D15, turn left to **Gordes★** (*i*🚶M♨️), a lively town with a good market. The plethora of craft shops attests to heavy tourist traffic. The Renaissance château (where Walk 2 ends and Walk 3 begins; photograph page 80) houses a Vasarely museum and the tourist office. But what you are most likely to remember about Gordes is its magnificent setting when seen from the south: it rises from the plateau like an acropolis. Watch for this view: it comes up *behind you* as you leave the village (photograph page 77).

Leave Gordes the way you came in — on the D15, then the D2*, following signs for CAVAILLON.

In **Coustellet** (♨️ and lavender **M**), you cross straight over the D900. The Petit Lubéron rises straight ahead.

*At **Robion** go straight over the first roundabout, then turn left at the second roundabout for LES TAILLADES (D31).*

The **Canal de Carpentras** is a

---

*To visit the Village des Bories (photograph page 79), go right under 100m from the roundabout where you joined the D2.

turquoise ribbon on your left, and you pass the **Moulin St-Pierre**, with a working water wheel.

When the D143 goes right to Cavaillon, follow CHEVAL-BLANC (still on the D31).

Attractive cane wind-breaks line both sides of the road, and the canal is still on your left.

Where the D234 goes right to Cavaillon, turn left and cross the canal.* Then turn left at the signpost for Vidauque, pass a restaurant on your right and, just beyond it turn sharp right (500m from the D31). Almost immediately you come to a Y-fork with a sign: FORET DOMANIALE DU LUBERON. Keep left uphill here; the road ahead is one-way for the next 5.5km.

Now climb the **Combe de Vidauque★** past various lay-bys (☞), including a fine viewpoint over Cavaillon at the foot of Mont St-Jacques (if you've ever tried to drive *through* Cavaillon, one of the largest market towns in France, you may agree with us that this is the best way to see it). The beautiful agricultural valley of the Durance glimmers below a backdrop of distant mountains. *Note:* the most impressive views of the Lubéron rising before you and the plain below come up during the first 3km of ascent, so pull up where you can before you climb too high. Almost before you notice it, the slumbering Lubéron springs to life: shaking off its green mantle, the mountain reveals rippling ribs of grey

limestone. If you come in spring, you'll find half the entries in your field guide to Mediterranean flora on this short stretch of road. You have climbed into an unbelievably beautiful rock garden, a rainbow of wild flowers.

The **Tête des Buisses** (619m) on the left marks the top of the climb (58km), and your descent begins ... down the 'Rat's Hole' (Le Trou-du-Rat). ***Beware: from here on this narrow road is two-way.*** Sweet-scented pines perfume the dramatic approach to the Durance Valley, where bamboos, conifers and poplars shield a cornucopia of cultivation beside the turquoise river. Just before the main road, you pass a shaded picnic area with a lovely brook, but no tables.

Cross the Canal de Carpentras and go left on the D973.

The heights of the Lubéron become more impressive again, as you head east, skirting the canal and passing the entrance to the **Gorges du Régalon** on the left.

Some 2km beyond Régalon turn right at the roundabout for MALLEMORT on the D32 and after 2km cross the Durance.

Entering **Bouches-du-Rhône**, the road is numbered D23.

Keep ahead to the D7N, then take the third exit off the roundabout for AIX.

Plane trees line one side of the road, cane the other; you cross the wide **Canal EDF**.

After 1.5km, at the roundabout, turn left on the D561, then follow ABBAYE DE SILVACANE.

Beyond **Charleval** (*i*) you cross the **Canal de Marseille** (wide turquoise canals are a

*In summer (dates fluctuate), the road route ahead will be closed, so keep on the D31, then turn left on the D973 and rejoin the tour at the Régalon Gorges.

The 'mushroom-stalks' of Saignon

prominent feature of this tour, as they were on Tour 1). As at Sénanque, the simplicity of the 12th-century Romanesque **Abbaye de Silvacane★** (92km ♣) is most impressive. St Bernard, who inspired the Cistercians, believed that saintliness could only come about through a life simply led, in poverty and isolation. All monastic buildings were to be pure in line and lacking in ornamentation. Think back to the isolated site of Sénanque; at its founding, Silvacane was equally isolated: this area was desolate, save for a 'forest of reeds' (*Sylva cana*).

From the abbey continue in the same direction. After 1.5km, go right for APT (D561). Just under 2km further on watch for your left turn for CADENET/APT (D543, easily missed).

Cross the **Canal EDF** and then the **Durance**, which is just a mass of pebbles here, and come into **Vaucluse** (where the road is renumbered D943). Enter **Cadenet** (98km ♣), where the 14/17th-century church has an attractive square 16th-century bell tower and interesting font.

Cross over the railway and keep following LOURMARIN, APT.

You bypass the centre of **Lourmarin** (*i*🏛♨). (But if you turn left into the village, seek out not only the 15/16th-century château, but the cemetery where Albert Camus is buried.) The vineyards, cherry orchards and stone houses around here are particularly attractive. Lourmarin is your next gateway into the Lubéron: from here you climb the **Combe de Lourmarin**, the wooded gorge of the Aigue-Brun River that splits the massif in two. To your left is the Petit Lubéron, renowned for its perched villages (Tour 4), to your right the Grand Lubéron, culminating in the peak of Mourre Nègre (1125m/3700ft).

After 6.5km turn left on the D36 for BONNIEUX. Exactly 3km along, turn left for the FORET DES CEDRES (small brown sign).

A nominal entrance/parking fee will be collected on your ascent. Just 3.3km uphill you pass a viewpoint on the right (📷; parking for one car *only*) — a superb picnic spot, from where there are tremendous, if often hazy, views down over Lacoste (left) and Bonnieux, surrounded by vineyards. When you reach the crest

(118km) the road ahead is closed to motor vehicles. This is the **Forêt des Cèdres**, shown on page 85 and, while there are no views, the aroma is enchanting. Walk 5 starts here, and we especially recommend Short walks 5-2 or 5-3.

Return to the D36 and go left towards BONNIEUX, but after just 300m turn right on the D232 for SAIGNON (may not be signed; very easily missed!).

This is another road with some bories, most on private property and some converted into 'bijou' residences.

At the D943, turn sharp right (not signed). Just 1.4km along turn sharp left for APT (D113).

A slender Romanesque tower, belonging to the recently restored 10th century priory of **St-Symphorien**, is seen straight ahead.

Just past the tower, turn right for BUOUX, immediately coming to a Y-fork, where you bear left. At the next junction go straight ahead for LES SEGUINS, FORT DE BUOUX.

Take the road up right to the substantial remains shown on page 81, the **Fort de Buoux** (□ destroyed in the 17th century by Louis XIV). When you return from the fort, head right for 300-400m to park for Walk 4.

Return to the U-turn of the D113 (450m back from parking for the fort) and bear right.

Climb steeply below more impressive rock walls draped with ivy. Beyond **Buoux** (✗) the tiny **Loube Valley** opens up on the right: one of our favourite views is the gorgeous farm to the right, just before crossing over the D232 (📷). Now wind downhill through

orchards. We are taking you into Apt and then out again immediately, to give you the best view of Saignon.

At a T-junction on the edge of Apt, turn right (the D22, not signed). After 300m turn left for DIGNE. Continue to a round-about on the D900, then take the first right, the D48 for SAIGNON VILLAGE.

There are some fine views★ (📷) over to **Saignon** as you approach the village, huddled below 'mushroom-stalks' of striated rock. The D48 turns right in front of Saignon, and you enjoy another superb view back to the village, focussing on the 12/16th-century church, as you climb above it.

Keep to the D48 beyond Saignon, first following AURIBEAU, then CASTELLET.

The road, in places hedged in by box and stone walls, now heads straight towards the Mourre Nègre. A few farmhouses with vineyards and herb gardens line the **Aigue-Brun Valley** on the right. Just before reaching the church in the lovely hamlet of **Auribeau**, the D48 turns left and snakes downhill with the Lubéron just on your right; on the left there are fine views towards St-Martin-de-Castillon on the far side of the **Calavon Valley**. Weave through **Castellet**, passing the hamlet's rusty old lavender still as you leave.

Turn left at a fork, cross the Calavon and turn left on the D900. Follow the D900 through Apt (AVIGNON, CAVAILLON) and, a few kilometres outside Apt, turn right on the D4 to Roussillon (166km).

Tour 3: MONT VENTOUX AND THE DENTELLES DE MONTMIRAIL

Roussillon • Sault • Mont Ventoux • Vaison-la-Romaine • Gigondas • Dentelles de Montmirail • Bédoin • l'Isle-sur-la-Sorgue (or Gorges de la Nesque • Roussillon)

182km/113mi; about 7-8h driving; Michelin map 332
Walks en route: 2, 6
Make an effort to get to Ventoux as early in the morning as possible; the heat haze builds up quickly, obscuring the wonderful views. The descent from Ventoux is a bit narrow at the start (unnerving for some drivers and passengers). No petrol from Sault to Malaucène (almost 50km on the tour). See the Alternative route on page 26 if you wish to return to Roussillon via the Gorges de la Nesque. Consider breaking the tour into two days, staying overnight at Vaison-la-Romaine.
Picnic suggestions: There are lovely shady picnic places where you can pull off the road on both the **southern and northern flanks of Ventoux**, but nothing to sit on (it can also be quite *cold* on the north side). At the bottom of the descent you pass the chapel of **Notre-Dame-du-Groseau**, the beautifully-kept chancel of an 11th-century Benedictine abbey, with stone seating round a shaded grassy 'court-yard' (parking on the left just beyond the chapel). The **Col du Cayron** in the Dentelles de Montmirail offers stones to sit on and shade. From the col you can turn right on a motorable track (behind a sign warning that you proceed at your own risk) to the Rocher du Midi viewpoint (⊼); or turn left and park below the St-Christophe chapel (see map and photographs on pages 87-88). Also **Roussillon** (see Car tour 1).

From the *table d'orientation* in Roussillon there is an enticing outlook towards Mont Ventoux rising almost due north. The summit, a sprawl of bare white limestone scree, looks snow-capped all year round. From a distance the mountain looks much higher than its 1909m/6262ft, because it rises in splendid isolation from the Carpentras and Vaucluse plains. And when you are on the summit, you will feel on top of the world — not only because of the panorama, but because of the bitter, icy-cold winds (*vents*) that buffet the peak. Take plenty of warm clothing, in case you want to venture out of the car! Be prepared for a drop in tem-

The surreal world at the summit of Mont Ventoux

perature of as much as 20°F (10°C), plus a high wind-chill factor. Later in the tour, you can stretch your legs in warmer surroundings, on the nearby Dentelles de Montmirail — the finely-etched 'lace' mountains.

*Leave **Roussillon** on the D227 for ST-SATURNIN, MURS, APT. Cross straight over the D4 and after 8km turn right on the D2. At the junction with the D943, turn sharp left for SAULT.*

The main tour passes to the left of **St-Saturnin-lès-Apt** (✝ and 15th-century gate). The D943 travels through *garrigues*, with some fine views left over the plain, where red daubs reveal Roussillon with the Lubéron stretching out behind it. The road skirts the deep **Urbane Valley** on the left, as you approach the **Plateau de Vaucluse**.

The plane-shaded château of **Javon** (▥) comes up as a surprise, here in the middle of nowhere, just beside the road. This fortified building is in mint condition. Some 6km further on there is a fine view of Ventoux ahead beyond fields. **St-Jean-de-Sault**, a pretty hamlet, is the next landmark, on your left. Now Ventoux is in sight all the time, rising off the striped cultivation of the plateau, where lavender predominates.

You cross the **river Croc**; Sault rises straight ahead on a rocky outcrop. Keep following SAULT and MONT VENTOUX, to go first right, then left, through **Sault** (39km *i*✝M⌂ and last ☕ for 50km), where there is a pleasant view from the terrace of the 12/14th-century Romanesque/Gothic church and a small museum of Gallo-Roman antiquities. Sault is an important centre on the 'Route de la Lavande'. Like the 'Route du Vin', this is a marketing

ploy, but a fairly well-defined swathe of blue and purple *does* extend across the Vaucluse Plateau from Vaison-la-Romaine all the way to Castel-lane (see *Landscapes of eastern Provence*). The cultivation of lavender was begun in the early 1900s in an attempt to slow the depopulation of this countryside; the crop adapted perfectly to the chalky soil.

*Javon (left); Notre-Dame-
d'Aubune (below left); bottom:
Mont Ventoux from the lavender
fields on the Plateau de Vaucluse*

come to the southern
viewpoint (■), with an
outlook stretching over your
base in the Lubéron and as far
as the Pyrenees. Then you pass
the relay station with its
souvenir shop and chapel and
descend to the northerly
viewpoint, from where you can
look out to the Alps and the
coast by Nice.

*From this viewpoint you
descend the north side of the
mountain in hairpin bends.*

The road is quite narrow in
places and not built up at the
side. On the first U-bend, just
by the observatory access road,
there is another fine view of the
Pyrenees.

*Keep left at two turn-offs to the
Mt Serein ski station, to stay on
the D974.*

You pass a viewpoint (□) on
the right over the **Ouvèze
Valley**. All the way down this
side of the mountain there are
gorgeous places under pines or
cypresses, for picnics on *very*
hot days! A better spot is
Notre-Dame-du-Groseau, on
your left after 85km (♠). This
holy place reputedly dates back
to pre-Celtic times, when a

*At a Y-fork, go left (slightly
downhill) for LE MT VENTOUX on
the D164, crossing the **Nesque**.*

Some 6km out of Sault there is
a fine view (□) back to the
left, down over Sault and the
cereal and lavender fields on
the plateau. You start to climb
Mont Ventoux through a
beautiful mixed forest. In June
plumes of yellow-flowering
laburnum light up the lower
slopes.
Beyond **Le Chalet-Reynard**
(■) the excellent road (now
the D974) climbs almost
effortlessly to the summit of
Mont Ventoux★ (65km),
where the *table d'orientation* is
split in two halves. First you

nearby spring was revered; if you picnic here, *please preserve the silence and leave **nothing** behind*.

At **Malaucène** (*i*♦💬⚖), the 14th-century church is built into the ramparts.

Entering Malaucène, turn right for GAP and VAISON (D938).

Vaison-la-Romaine★ (95km *i*🎪♦M⚖), an exquisite small town, rose above the Ouvèze as a Celtic *oppidum*, but came under Roman control in the 2nd century BC. If nothing else, visit the extensive Roman ruins. An overnight stop would enable you to take in other sights, including the museum displaying finds from excavations in the area.

Leave Vaison on the D977 for AVIGNON. After some 5km, at the roundabout, take the third exit for SEGURET (D88) and keep left at a Y-fork for SEGURET and ROUTE DES VINS.

The D88 passes below **Séguret**, where a ruined castle rises up on the left.

At the roundabout below the village, take the first exit, the D23 for SABLET.

Soon mellow **Sablet** is a pyramid in front of you, with its church at the apex.

At the roundabout outside Sablet, take the third exit for GIGONDAS (D7) and keep left immediately at a Y-fork.

Gigondas is famous for its red Grenache wine.

Approaching Gigondas, fork left for GIGONDAS and LES FLORETS on the D79. Then follow LES FLORETS and DEN-TELLES DE MONTMIRAIL, leaving Gigondas off to the right.

One of the larger water wheels in L'Isle-sur-la-Sorgue

The lovely road (D229) climbs through vineyards towards the **Dentelles de Montmirail**★, and there's a fine view ahead of the range's jagged crown. The climb ends at the **Col du Cayron** (113km), at the foot of the Dentelles Sarrasines, the most northerly of the two chains and the 'lacier'. Walk 6 starts here and takes you up, over and round the crests. Short walk 6 is particularly rewarding and would take you to the rock pillars shown on page 87 in just half an hour.

Return the way you came and, back at the D79, follow AUTRES DIRECTIONS, then keep following VACQUEYRAS (D80, D7).

You pass several *dégustations*, eventually edging **Vaqueyras** on the D7 (the centre is off to the left). Continuing south, the lovely Romanesque bell tower of **Notre-Dame-d'Aubune** is seen up to the left (♦).

Fork left for BEAUMES (D81).

At the T-junction turn left into lovely **Beaumes-de-Venise** (*i🏠*). Keep the church on your left.

Just past the church, turn left on the D90 for LAFARE. You will now follow the D90 all the way to Malaucène.

You pass a pretty chapel on the right. In **Lafare** continue straight ahead for SUZETTE. Along this stretch there are several good viewpoints back to the Dentelles (📷): just past a turn-off left to Château Neuf, pull up on the right to see the two parallel ridges side-on. From this angle the Grand Montmirail (on the left) looks just as razor-sharp as the Dentelles Sarrasines. This view is at its best early in the day, but makes a dramatic afternoon silhouette.

Go through **Suzette** and turn left for *MALAUCENE*. Some 4km along you come to the **Col de la Chaîne** (📷; '472m' on the Michelin map). From here

there is another superb side-on view back to the Dentelles and ahead to the lower flanks of Ventoux. Descend across a many-hued palette of cultivation, heading straight for Ventoux, until you come back to **Malaucène** (139km).

Follow VILLAGE-CENTRE through the plane-shaded esplanade and then keep straight ahead on the D938 for BEDOIN and CARPENTRAS (where Ventoux is signposted to the left). Just 3km past the sign denoting the exit from Malaucène, turn left on the D19 for BEDOIN.

Beyond a small lake on the right, you climb past clipped hedges and low pines to a grassy moorland. Under 3km along, the **Belvédère du Paty** comes up on the right (📷): from here you look out over the plain, with the Lubéron (left) and the Alpilles (right) in the distance. Ventoux is ahead and to the left. Below, at

GORGES DE LA NESQUE: ALTERNATIVE RETURN TO ROUSSILLON

In Bédoin follow MT VENTOUX on the D974, but at a Y-fork outside the village, ignore the D974 climbing Ventoux from the south; keep on the D19 to **Flassan***, an ochre-coloured village. At the crossroads in Flassan turn right for VILLES-SUR-AUZON (still D19, badly signposted). In* **Villes** *join the one-way system at first, then carefully follow SAULT and GORGES DE LA NESQUE (D942).*

The attractive *but sometimes narrow* road travels through holm oaks and manicured box hedges (⌂) above the deep **Gorges de la Nesque** on the right. Fold after fold of mountain creeps out of hiding in the gorge ahead. About 12km from Villes you look towards the most impressive part of the gorge, where high vertical grey-rock walls rise sheer from the river. From now on there is a good run of *belvédères* (📷); the best are after the first and third tunnels — from the latter you look across to the massive abutment of the **Rocher du Cire** and up the gorge towards Mont Ventoux. Beyond here the gorge flattens out into the verdant swathe of the Nesque Valley.

After passing below a 12th-century tower at **Monieux**, keep right for SAULT, crossing the plateau, a tapestry of lavender and cereals.

When you meet the D1 left to Villes, head right into **Sault***; from there follow ST-SATURNIN, to return to* **Roussillon** *on your outgoing route (231km).*

---

picturesque Crillon-le-Brave, the clay quarries exude ochre hues.

Bédoin (151.5km *i♟*), a gorgeous perched village, has an 18th-century classical church. From Bédoin we head south to l'Isle-sur-la-Sorgue, but see the Alternative above if you prefer to return to Roussillon via the Gorges de la Nesque.

Follow CARPENTRAS through Bédoin and outside the village, heading south on the D974. You pass the large Ventoux wine co-operative on the right.

Some 5.5km from Bédoin go left for MAZAN on the D163.

As the road squeezes into **Mazan** (*i♟*), it is worth turning right to visit the 12th-century church, where there is a wall built from 62 sarcophagi which once lined the Roman road between Sault and Carpentras.

26

Otherwise turn left on a wide street, then follow PERNES (D1).

Climbing out of the **Auzon Valley**, there are fine views back to the Dentelles, Ventoux, and east to the Montagne de Lure. The road crosses the D4 and then the **Canal de Carpentras**.

At the roundabout outside Pernes go left for ISLE-SUR-LA-SORGUE on the D938, crossing the Nesque immediately and then curving right.

Pernes-les-Fontaines (172km *i♟*) is a charming small town with many fountains, an 11th-century church, and a chapel, bridge and gate dating from the 16th century. But **L'Isle-sur-la-Sorgue★** (182km; *i♺* and 17th-century *♟*) is *really* special, on account of the beautiful teal-green Sorgue River, the tree-lined avenues, and the dozen or so lovely old water wheels — still working.

Tour 4: THE THREE-STAR ROUTE

L'Isle-sur-la-Sorgue • Fontaine-de-Vaucluse • Oppède-le-Vieux • Bonnieux • Avignon • Pont du Gard

124km/77mi; about 4h driving; Michelin map 332

Walks en route: 7. Walks 4, 5, 8 and 11 are nearby; Walks 9 and 10 are easily reached from Remoulins (near the Pont du Gard).

The ideal way to do this tour is to set out no later than 8am, to be at the Fontaine de Vaucluse before the crowds. Leave there by 9am and potter about the Lubéron (Walks 4-5), getting to Avignon late in the day, to break the tour. Spend the next day at Avignon and arrive at the Pont du Gard in the early evening. If you have only one day, you can still see the highlights of Avignon during the afternoon.

Picnic suggestions: The **Pont Julien**, a Roman bridge, is crossed halfway through the tour. You can sit on rocks beside the river Calavon; there is shade nearby. At the end of the tour the banks of the Gardon on either side of the **Pont du Gard** make idyllic picnic spots.

T his short tour takes in not only two of the most popular tourist attractions in Provence, but some of the finest perched villages in the Lubéron. *Do* set out early, to have these landscapes (almost) to yourself.

From **L'Isle-sur-la-Sorgue** *take the D938 north (CARPENTRAS, FONTAINE-DE-VAUCLUSE). Cross the Sorgue and in just under 1km, at the roundabout, take the first exit for FONTAINE-DE-VAUCLUSE (D25).*

You pass under an aqueduct and approach **Fontaine-de-Vaucluse★** (7km *i✝□M*). Coming into the main square, turn left to the signposted 'parking', just as you approach the central column, dedicated to Petrarch. Now set off on foot to the famous source (shown overleaf): from the column take the tarmac lane at the left of the 'Glacier'. You enter a magnificent *cirque*, below which the Sorgue rushes by on your right. After a climb of 15-20 minutes, the path ends at a chaos of gigantic

The famous Pont d'Avignon, in winter

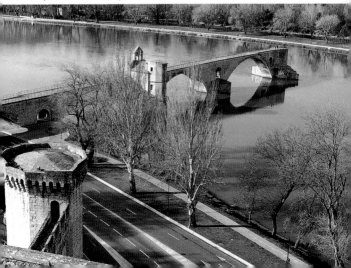

boulders. In summer or early autumn all you will see is a tiny pool of murky turquoise water. It is hard to believe that this is one of the most powerful springs in the world! But in winter, when the vast underground reservoir in the bowels of the Vaucluse Plateau is full of rainwater, it's a different story — a deluge of emerald green water roars *over* the boulders.

Linger a while beside the rushing river, where Petrarch sought peace of mind and inspiration. When the first day-trippers snake into view, walk back to the village and take a look at the 11th-century Romanesque church of St-Véran, the old water wheel, and the derelict mills.

Leave Fontaine-de-Vaucluse by following TOUTES DIRECTIONS from the square. After just 300m, at a Y-fork, bear left on a narrow lane (not signposted).

This road, the D100a, is the 'Touristic Route to Gordes'. It affords a good view back left to the *cirque* above the Fontaine de Vaucluse.

Meeting the D100 at a T-junction, go left for CABRIERES and GORDES.

Soon come to the **Belvédère du Tête du Soldat** on the right (📷🍴), overlooking Lagnes just below, the Alpilles and the Lubéron. Further on you pass a monument to the Resistance (🍴), from where a footpath leads east to Cabrières and the 'Mur de la Peste' (see panel on page 79).

At the next fork bear left, to squeeze through lovely **Cabrières-d'Avignon**. *From here to Oppède, care is needed to follow the convoluted roads. Go right and right again immediately (where a left turn is signed to 'Les Cedres').*

The Lubéron stretches straight in front of you now.

At a Y-fork, go right for CAVAILLON, passing a shrine on the left. Cross the D15 and, at the roundabout, take the second exit for ROBION, CAVAILLON, COUSTELLET (D2).

In **Coustellet** (M) you pass the Lavender Museum on your left.

Top: walking to the Fontaine de Vaucluse we pass this 13th-century castle and three museums — dedicated to Vaucluse speleology, the Resistance, and traditional paper-making methods. At the paper museum there is a fine viewing platform over the Sorgue. Bottom: at the source

Pont Julien (right) and church at Oppède-le-Vieux (below)

Go straight over the D900 and, 1.5km further on, turn left for MAUBEC, MENERBES (D144). Just 0.4km further on, go left on the D3 (MENERBES, BONNIEUX, OPPEDE).

On the right, vineyards spread out below the Petit Lubéron.

Be sure to turn right, 1.5km further on, for LES LONES (D176), ignoring the sign for Oppède straight ahead. Then, after just 0.3km, bear right at a Y-fork for OPPEDE-LE-VIEUX. Cross the D29 and go straight over for OPPEDE-LE-VIEUX; ignore the left turn to the village of Oppède.

The lovely lane heads straight for the mountain.
Leave your transport in the designated car park below **Oppède-le-Vieux★** (21km ♣☐📷) and climb through the old gateway to the upper village. From both the ruined 15/16-century castle and the church (13th century, but twice rebuilt) there are fine views.

When you leave the car park, turn right downhill (D178). Just over 1.5km along, at the roundabout, take the first exit for MENERBES (D188), then keep following MENERBES.

Eventually Ménerbes rises dramatically to your left, spread along a ridge.

Curve round in a U-turn below the village then, at a T-junction, go right for BONNIEUX. At another T-junction, go left for Ménerbes CENTRE.

As you climb through **Ménerbes★** (♣☐📷), fork left (EGLISE, MAIRIE). Then fork right uphill for EGLISE, MAIRIE. When you come to the *mairie*,

flags aflutter, pull over right to a viewpoint encompassing the plain, Gordes, Roussillon, the Plateau de Vaucluse, and Mont Ventoux. Then walk on to visit the 12th-century church at the end of the road.

Returning from the viewpoint in the one-way system, fork lef at the first opportunity (not signposted; rue de la Fontaine). Then go left again at the next Y-fork (with a parking area below to your left). Meeting the D3, cross over on the D109 for LACOSTE.

You cross the **river Réal** and pass the road to the **Abbaye St-Hilaire** on the right. The road runs through *garrigues* now, and you look straight ahead to the Mourre Nègre on the Grand Lubéron, with its relay station.
Come into **Lacoste** (☐ and 17th century ♣), where the ruined château of the infamous Marquis de Sade and his family rises on the left. There is a fantastic view over the colourfully-cultivated patchwork of the Bonnieux plain straight ahead.

Just 0.5km after the sign for Lacoste, at a T-junction, turn sharp right for BONNIEUX (D109), leaving the village centre off to your right. After just over 3km, at a T-junction, turn left for BONNIEUX (D3).

The village rises ahead in a pyramid, with the church at the apex (☎). **Bonnieux★** (46km *i❄*☐☎ and bakery **M**), the last of the perched villages en route, also boasts superb views — from the terrace in the centre, near the 12th-century church.

Leave Bonnieux for GOULT (D194). (But to get to Walk 4 or 5, take the D36 south towards LOURMARIN.) Keep following GOULT but, 3.3km from the roundabout in Bonnieux (just past an electricity transformer on the right that doubles as a dovecot), turn right for ROUSSILLON (D108). Continue to a roundabout and take the third exit, to park for Pont Julien.

Pont Julien★ (**🎋**), a 1st-century bridge with three graceful arches, supported the Via Domitia on its way south from Sisteron and Apt.

*Return to the roundabout and take the exit for ROUSSILLON, crossing the **Calavon**. Immediately joining the D900, turn left. This road (later D901) will take you almost all the way to the Pont du Gard. Keep following ISLE-SUR-LA-SORGUE and, from there, AVIGNON.*

Beyond L'Isle-sur-la-Sorgue, you come into **Le Thor** (*i❄*).

At a roundabout near the centre, take the first exit for AVIGNON.

As the road curves left, look right to see the splendidly extravagant bell-cage over the village gate. (Or detour 3km

north here: go right, *through* the gate, on the D16, to see the fine stalactites in the Grotte de Thouzon. En route you pass Le Thor's 13th-century Romanesque church with Gothic vaulting.)

At **Avignon★** (94km *i❄*☐✕**M** ☎♨) you leave the cradle of the Durance for the mighty Rhône. The best place to park is at the railway station (follow GARE). If you are on a tight schedule, just climb the Rocher des Doms (viewing table). From there you can take in the ramparts, palaces, churches and bridges in one fell swoop — to say nothing of the surrounding and far-off countryside. If you *do* have the time to spend here, our guide *Walk and Eat Around Avignon* would show you the best of this vibrant city.

*Leave Avignon for NIMES, ALES (N100) and cross the **Rhône**. At a roundabout where the D976 comes in from the right (after 14km) turn left for REMOULINS. The Pont du Gard is well sign-posted from **Remoulins** (120km). Either follow RIVE GAUCHE (major parking area/exhibition centre) or RIVE DROITE (parking, restaurant, shops). **You can not cross the bridge by car; each entrance is a cul-de-sac.***

The **Pont du Gard★** (124km *i🎋*✕**M**; see pages 42-43; Walk 7) is a UNESCO World Heritage Site, with exhibitions and tourist facilities. But the area has not been spoilt — the landscape has been cleared of motor traffic and everything that previously detracted from the monument. The site is *very* crowded during the day, but if you arrive late, the crowds will have gone. The memory of an evening picnic beside the river would stay with you forever.

Tour 5: ANTIQUITIES AND THE ALPILLES

Pont du Gard • Nîmes • Tarascon • Les Baux-de-Provence • St-Rémy-de-Provence • Glanum • (Avignon) • Villeneuve-lès-Avignon • (Orange) • Pont du Gard

198km/123mi; about 6-7h driving; Michelin map 340
Walks en route: 7, 8, 11-13. Walk 14 is just a short detour away, and Walks 9 and 10 are easily reached from Remoulins near the Pont du Gard.
Good, but busy roads. To visit Nîmes and just touch on nearby Avignon or Orange, you will need at least two days. If you plan to do the tour in one day and walk as well, save Nîmes for another day and take this pretty route: after Pont St-Nicolas turn left on the D135 and follow it via Poulx and Marguerittes to the D999. Pick up the tour again on the approach to Beaucaire. A base near the Pont du Gard or Remoulins is also ideal for visiting the Cèze and Ardèche gorges by nipping north on the D6086 (even the Ardèche is only an hour away), so we have included walks
at each of these popular beauty spots (Walks 9 and 10).
Picnic suggestions: Halfway through the tour there are several picnic places with pleasant views. If you drive just 200m past the **Le Destet** turn-off, there is a shaded picnic spot on the left beside a wide irrigation canal. Perch on the side of the canal if you have no chairs. The **D24 from Le Destet to Eygalières** offers excellent pine-shaded picnic spots by the roadside. You can sit on the wall at the **St-Sixte** chapel (photograph pages 36-37; limited shade). A popular spot with local people is the pine-shaded lake just south of **St-Rémy**, where Walk 12 begins (see 'How to get there' on page 104 and photograph page 105). Also, of course, the **Pont du Gard**.

This tour captures the essence of Provence, its history, landscape and flavour. Apart from seeing many of the most impressive Roman remains in the country, we visit Glanum, settled as early as 500BC but then overrun by the Barbarians, and Les Baux, court of the troubadours. Plane tree avenues and flat market gardens hedged in by graceful windbreaks provide the perfect foil for the glaring-white limestone massif of the Alpilles. Leave the car and every footstep crushes out a new heady aroma. *Ah! Ça sent la Provence!*

The Alpilles from the D24 near the junction with the D24b to Eygalières

Leave from the left bank of the
Pont du Gard *(the north side*
of the bridge), taking the D981
northwest towards UZES. After
3.5km go left on the D112 for
COLLIAS and, under 2.5km
along, turn left on the D3, still
following COLLIAS.

You pass a pleasant grove of
poplars (⊼) and cross the
Alzon; on the right there is a
lovely weir.

Walk 8, based on **Collias** (ᗺᗷ),
runs through a nature reserve
on the banks of the Gardon
(photographs pages 93-94).

From Collias take the D112 via
SANILHAC.

You will pass a menhir on the
left. In spring the young leaves
of the cherry trees glow rosy-
red in the morning sun.

On meeting the D979 go left for
NIMES and PONT ST-NICHOLAS.

You cross the **Gardon** on a
very narrow, wiggly 13th-
century bridge with nine arches
at **Pont St-Nicholas**, a pretty
hamlet. Once over it, go left;
with luck you will find space to
tuck in beyond the bridge, to
walk back and admire the
setting and the gorgeous green
river. Then go through the
Gorges du Gardon.

(Now, to avoid Nîmes, turn left
for Poulx on the D135.)

It is essential to have a street
plan to hand as you enter
Nîmes★ (32km *i*⌂**▯**✕M ᗺᗷ)
— there is a good plan in our
guide, *Walk and Eat Around*
Avignon, which also describes a
day-long walking tour in lovely
Nîmes. But if you are pressed
for time, park in the northern
part of the city, off Avenue
Jean Jaurès, by the Jardins de la
Fontaine. A visit to these
exquisite 18th-century gardens
and fountains (in Roman times

fed by water from the Pont du
Gard) is a must. The Tour
Magne, at the top of the
gardens, was part of a pre-
Roman line of defenses. From
the gardens walk south along
Boulevard Victor Hugo, stop
at the tourist office on your
left, and then take in the three
principal 'sights': the Maison
Carrée, Lord Foster's Carré
d'Art opposite, and the arena
further south.

Head east from Nîmes on the
D999, and keep following
BEAUCAIRE, TARASCON at all
the roundabouts.

At **Beaucaire**★ (55km *i*⌂M ᗺᗷ)
the road runs beside the **Canal**
du Rhône à Sète — a very
attractive stretch. You may
wish to see the remains of the
11/13th-century castle (▭),
which houses a museum of
local history, including docu-
ments about the famous Beaucaire Fair. In medieval times as
many as 300,000 people took
part in these festivities in the
course of a week. The fair was
launched in 1217 by Raymond
VI, Count of Toulouse (who
figures prominently in the
history of the Cathars; see
panel page 62).

If you are not stopping at
Beaucaire, continue across the
Rhône to the twin city of
Tarascon★ (*i*✝**▯**). The
approach is magnificent: the
seven towers of the massive
13/15th-century château, one
of the finest medieval castles in
France, rise majestically above
the wide, fast-flowing river.
Almost adjacent to the bridge
is the 9/14th-century church of
Ste-Marthe, which was greatly
damaged during Allied air
attacks on bridges over the
Rhône.

After driving over the bridge,

Jardins de la Fontaine at Nîmes

follow CAVAILLON/ARLES/ ST-REMY/CENTRE VILLE over a roundabout and then along lovely plane tree-shaded avenues. Keep on this road (D99), following ST-REMY.

Soon you can see the Alpilles ahead — slightly to the right. After crossing the D570n, almost at once you come into one of those fantastic plane-tree avenues which characterise this tour. Together with cane and cypresses, they protect the market gardens here from the *mistral.*

*Some 2.5km past the round-about at the exit from **Mas-Blanc-des-Alpilles**, turn right on the D27 for LES BAUX.*

Soon you're climbing through aromatic pines and *maquis.*

Just over 5.5km uphill, watch for a tarmac firefighters' lane off right (AL109); immediately beyond it turn left on another narrow lane (AL110). (These firefighters' lanes are often redesignated, so may be numbered differently in future.)

After 0.6km the tar ends; park and walk up left for breath-taking views over Les Baux and to the Camargue, the Rhône Valley, the Lubéron and Mont Ventoux (☎). But you may not be sure what you're looking at: the once lovely, tiled *table d'orientation* that was here for years has been vandalised — chiselled off its base! Short walk 12-2 starts here (photo-graph pages 106-107).

Return to the D27 and turn left.

Park at the entrance to **Les Baux-de-Provence★** (76km *i*⬜✕**M**). Although at the heart of the Alpilles, Les Baux rises on a completely detached spur, with sheer escarpments on all sides; the site is extraordinary. Sadly but inevitably, today the village is so commercialised that there is no enjoyment jostling through the alleyways and ruins. If you are staying nearby overnight, try to get here first thing in the morning, although you will not be let into the ancient citadel until the gates open (9am). Walk 12 comes into the village below some of the old bauxite mines, which were opened in the early 1820s and gave rise to the modern aluminium industry. *Leave Les Baux on the D27 for MAUSSANE.*

The area around **Maussane-les-Alpilles** (♒) is olive country, and Walk 13 would plunge you into the heart of the sizzling olive groves.

The main tour now heads east from Maussane, to the Alpilles.

(But if you first want to see Daudet's mill★, a detour of 18km return, take the D17 to Fontvieille, then go left on the D33 in the centre of the village. From Fontvieille you can continue 4km west on the D17 to the 12th-century Chapelle Ste-Croix and Benedictine

Abbaye de Montmajour★.
Return to Maussane to
continue.)

From Maussane head first
towards MOURIES on the D17,
but after 0.2km turn left on the
D5 for EYGALIERES. Then, about
0.6km along the D5, turn left
again on the D78 to LE DESTET
(badly signposted).

This is one of the prettiest
roads in Provence. The flat
road skirts to the south of the
crumpled white limestone
Chaîne des Alpilles★.
Espaliered fruit trees, olive
groves, vineyards and the
occasional flock of sheep in the
road add character and colour
to this thirsty landscape. You
pass the Mas de Gourgonnier
on the left, surrounded by
vineyards and olive groves.

At a T-junction with the D24,
turn left for EYGALIERES. (But to
park for Walk 13 or to have a
picnic, turn right for 0.2km,
then turn left on a track with a
sign for the Vaudoret olive oil
mill. A wide irrigation channel
is ahead to the right.)

Heading towards Eygalières,
pass the pretty hamlet of **Le**
Destet and continue on the
gorgeous pine-shaded road,
bright with broom in spring,
with views of the Alpilles to
the left. Descending out of the
pines, you enjoy a lovely
outlook to the foothills, with
vineyards in foreground.

Les Baux-de-Provence, with the
ruined castle at the far left. In the
13th century this fortified town was
renowned as a court of love and
visited by the troubadours. But in
the 14th century it was in the
hands of Raymond de Turenne —
viscount by birth, but kidnapper by
trade. When no payment was
forthcoming, his victims were hurled
from the castle into the abyss below.

At the junction with the D25,
turn left for EYGALIERES,
keeping on the D24. (But to
park for Walk 14, a splendid
excursion to a Saracen tower,
go right, then right again on
the D25A to AUREILLE (✕⌖).)

You head straight for the Alpilles, passing several *domaines*.

Beyond the Vallonge vineyards,
turn right for EYGALIERES on the
D24B (photograph page 31).

Eygalières (97.5km ⌖), once
a Neolithic settlement, rises in
terraces on a hilltop at the left
of the road. Keep on D24b; a
sign reminds you that the
Resistance fighter Jean Moulin
sheltered near here in January
1942. You pass the 12th-
century **Chapelle St-Sixte** on
the right (✝; photograph
overleaf), crowning a low hill.
The road is flanked by
beautiful Provençal farms and
fields, with mountains rising in
the far distance.

Some 3.4km from the chapel a
lane off left is signposted to the
Valditon vineyards. Ignore this,

but turn left on another lane just 100m beyond it (also signed to VALDITON).

You pass another entrance to this *domaine* and, keeping left at an unsigned Y-fork, cross the **Canal des Alpilles**. The bamboo and cypresses used as windbreaks here are a delight.
Go straight over the D73ᴇ and turn left on the main D99 road.

Soon planes arch over the road — the same shady cathedral of trees that you first entered at Mas-Blanc-des-Alpilles some 15km to the west! Through the trees you look left across gentle farmlands, where row upon row of cypress and poplar windbreaks stand out darkly against the white-lace chalk of the Alpilles.
After 10.5km turn left for ST-REMY/LES ANTIQUES/GLANUM.

Although there is nothing of great architectural importance in **St-Rémy-de-Provence★** (116km *i✗M♨*), it merits a star for its atmosphere — all light and shade, the real flavour

of Provence — with plane-shaded squares, fountains and intriguing lanes. St-Rémy was founded after the destruction of Glanum, from which important archaeological finds reside in the museum at the Hôtel de Sade.

Leave St-Rémy on the D5 for LES BAUX.

You pass the tourist office on your right. If you plan to do Walk 12 or you would like to picnic by the lake shown on page 105, keep an eye open now for a turn-off right just 0.6km past the tourist office: there is a small sign, *LAC 'DES PIEROOU', BARRAGE*. Otherwise pull up on the right 0.5km beyond this turn-off, at **Les Antiques★** (**π**), a mausoleum and the triumphal arch shown overleaf — the surviving remains of the wealthy Roman city of Glanum, which was overrun by the Barbarians in the 3rd century and abandoned. Short walk 12-2 comes in here, heading for St-Rémy.

Above: the triumphal arch at Les Antiques; right: the 12th-century Chapelle St-Sixte — an idyllic picnic spot, with fine views to Eygalières and the Alpilles.

Just over the road are the **Glanum excavations ★ (ⁱⓣ✕)**, covering about five acres. The area is thought to have been first settled by Celtic-Ligurian peoples (Glanics) in the 6th century BC, at the site of a sacred spring. Later building was carried out by the Greeks and then the Romans. Adjacent to Glanum is **St-Paul de Mausole**, where Van Gogh was hospitalised; see notes about this area on page 104 (Short walk 12-2), and photograph on page 108.

*Return from here to **St-Rémy** and then head west on the D99 for TARASCON and BEAUCAIRE. After 10.5km, at a roundabout, take the first exit, the D570N for AVIGNON. (The third exit leads to Arles after 13km.)*

La Montagnette, a 'mini-Alpilles', is seen ahead.

After 7km take the third exit from the roundabout (D970 for TARASCON, BEAUCAIRE); then, just 0.6km further on, bear left on a slip road (D81 for BARBENTANE, ABBAYE DE FRIGOLET).

You circle over the D970 and the railway, heading across **La Montagnette**, where pines and olives vie for space. As you climb in hairpins, an impressively sited 19th-century pilgrimage abbey, **St-Michel-de-Frigolet** (✕), rises out of

36

nowhere. The austere 19th-century spires seen on the approach are not very appealing, but inside the lavishly decorated main church you'll find the original 11th- century abbey (N-D-du-Bon-Remède), now an apse off the north aisle. Take some time to wander along the shaded cobbled walkways, past the simple 12th-century church of St Michel — and perhaps have tea and cake in the café. You could start Walk 11 here, instead of in Barbentane.

Follow BARBENTANE (D35ᴇ) from the abbey.

In **Barbentane** (*i*⫿✕♨) you will see the exquisite château shown on page 100. Unfortunately it's no longer open to the public. Walk 11 starts at Barbentane.

Follow the one-way system west out of Barbentane, signed to BOULBON via the D35. After some 3km take the second exit from the roundabout, the D402 (ST-PIERRE/MEZOARGUES/VALLA-BREGUES) and cross the Rhône.

This handy bridge in the middle of nowhere avoids the afternoon traffic in Tarascon and Beaucaire and takes you to

an equally handy road — the D2.

Turn right on the D2.

You skirt the Rhône, with good views to Avignon. The castellated walls of **Villeneuve-lès-Avignon★** (*i*✝♜⚖📷) once enclosed the summer palaces of Agignon's cardinals. Visit the 14th-century monastery (Chartreuse du Val de Bénédiction) and Fort St-André with its impressive gate. Then climb the Tour de Philippe le Bel for some of the most beautiful views on the tour, as the low sun burns out over Avignon, the Rhône and the Pont Bénézet. Ventoux is visible in the north, and you can trace all of the day's route through the Alpilles and La Montagnette.

From Villeneuve continue north on the D980 for BAGNOLS and then ROQUEMAURE.

Beyond **Sauveterre** planes and poplars protect the orchards and fields lining the road.

At the second roundabout on the Roquemaure ring road, take the third exit, the D976 for NIMES. (By taking the first exit, you could detour north for 11km to Orange★ (Π⚖), to see the triumphal arch which once stood on the Via Agrippa to Arles and the best-preserved Roman theatre in existence.)

In **Roquemaure** (13th-century ✝) follow NIMES and the one-way system to keep to the D976. Quickly passing the chapel of **St-Joseph**, carry on through vineyards backed by wrinkled limestone hills.

Go straight over the D6580 roundabout, following NIMES.

You skirt the famous Tavel rosé vineyards for the next 5km! There is a viewing terrace (📷) at **Notre-Dame-de-Grâce**, an almshouse up to your right, built on the site of a Benedictine priory. The road then passes to the right of pretty **Rochefort-du-Gard**. Soon the landscape deteriorates into suburbia.

At the N100 roundabout take the first exit (NIMES/REMOULINS/PONT DU GARD).

Cresting a rise, you have an excellent view along the valley of the Gardon towards Uzès.

*From **Remoulins** see page 30 at the 120km-point, to continue to the **Pont du Gard** (198km), remembering that **you can not drive across the bridge!***

Tour 6: THE CAMARGUE AND ARLES

Pont du Gard • Beaucaire • St-Gilles • Aigues-Mortes • Stes-Maries-de-la-Mer • Digue à la Mer • Plage de Piémanson • Arles • Pont du Gard

278km/172mi; about 8h driving; Michelin map 339
Walks en route: 7, 15
This is a two-day tour: on day 1 see the Camargue, then stay overnight in Arles, devoting the next day to its wealth of sights. Some roads in the Camargue are very narrow; be prepared, too, for cars in front to come to a halt without warning (the occupants have spotted some birds). The only petrol stations en route in the

Camargue are at Stes-Maries and Salin.
Picnic suggestions: Shade is hard to come by in the Camargue, and (in our experience) most areas are plagued by biting insects. If you have a beach umbrella, the daisy-encrusted dunes at the **Plage de Piémanson** make an idyllic beach setting, unless it's very windy.

The Camargue, a vast plain, is the result of a remorseless battle waged over millions of years between the silt deposits in the Rhône Delta and the salty waters of the Mediterranean. Man imposed a fragile truce in the latter part of the 19th century, when the waters of the Rhône were channelled and a sea wall built (Digue à la Mer). From the Camargue we follow the Grand Rhône north to Arles, the finest Roman city in Provence and a Mecca for van Gogh enthusiasts. Wander the alleys in the evening; with luck the lamplight will fall upon an Arlésienne in her red and white costume, her bell-clear voice singing Bizet's haunting theme.

*From **Pont du Gard** drive to **Remoulins**, then take the D6086 for NIMES, BEAUCAIRE, TARASCON. A a fork, go left on the D986L for BEAUCAIRE and TARASCON, leaving the D6086 for Nîmes off to the right.*

After some 12km, skirting the Rhône, there is a view to the enormous **Barrage de Vallabrègues** on the left. See Car tour 5 (page 32) for brief notes about **Beaucaire** (22km).

From Beaucaire take the D38 for ST-GILLES.

Outside **Bellegarde** the D38 skirts the **Canal du Rhône**, before taking you into **St-Gilles** (48km *i✝*). The west front of the 11/12-century

abbey church is a masterpiece of medieval sculpture. St-Gilles was home to the powerful Counts of Toulouse, who built up a vast domain and led crusades to the Holy Land. But when Pope Innocent III's envoy was murdered at St-Gilles in 1208, blame fell upon the then count, Raymond VI. He was excommunicated and forced to mount another crusade — against the Cathars (see panel page 62). As a humanist who had always tolerated the heretics, Raymond soon rebelled against these orders.

Follow STES-MARIES-DE-LA-MER to head southeast on the D6572

38

but, soon after crossing the canal, fork right on the D179.

The **Ecluse de St-Gilles** is the lock that controls the canal between the Petit Rhône and the Canal du Rhône à Sète. Now you're in Haut or 'upper' Camargue, where desalination and fresh-water irrigation from the Rhône allow the cultivation of numerous crops, including wheat, vines, and fruit. Beyond **La Fosse** rice paddies dominate the landscape — the chief crop in the region, since it can withstand slightly salty water. At **Mas des Iscles** the D179 turns left beside the **Canal des Capettes**.

Just past **Montcalm** (18th-century ▯), where flowering fields paint bold colours onto this muted canvas in spring, the road runs into the D58 at a roundabout. Some 8km further on you cross the **Canal du Rhône à Sète**.

Just beyond the canal, take the first exit off the roundabout (D46).

From the 14th-century **Tour Carbonnière**, a watchtower on the old salt road (♜📷), you can look out over Aigues-Mortes and as far north as the Cévennes.

Return to the roundabout and take the second exit for AIGUES-MORTES (D46).

Allow at least two hours to visit **Aigues-Mortes**★ (81km ***i***). The fascinating (and gruesome) history of this 13th-century fortified town (when its population was almost four times what it is today and the sea was more easily accessible) will keep you spellbound. Visit the ramparts and the Constance Tower (♜📷), and imagine the pageantry in 1248, when St-Louis embarked on his crusades with 35,000 men in 1500 chartered ships!

From Aigues-Mortes return to the roundabout just before Montcalm and, ignoring the first exit (to an hotel), keep on the D58 for STES-MARIES. Some 5km further on, go right on the D38 for STES-MARIES.

The history of **Stes-Maries-de-la-Mer**★ (110.5km; 12th-century Romanesque fortified ✝ and ***i***⚖) is steeped in legend, and for centuries it has been a place of pilgrimage, especially for gypsies. But modern-day travellers' camps being no more appealing in Stes-Maries than anywhere else, we are always glad to move on.

Drive back north on the D570.

Lime-green rice paddies glimmer along both sides of the road. At the **Pont-de-Gau Bird Sanctuary** you can see some of the nearly 400 different birds identified in the area. The **Camargue Natural Regional Park**★ was created in 1970, partly to protect the delta from an undisciplined spread of low-grade tourist facilities; its Information Centre (***i***) is beside the **Ginès Lagoon**.

Some 22km north of Stes-Maries turn right on the D37 for SALIN.

Montcalm makes a pleasant picture in spring.

Top: rice paddies (clos) are flooded between April and September; they make a chequerboard of glassy pools, framed by poplars. Below: salt-encrusted surface algae and wooden retaining posts (ganivelles) create beautiful abstract patterns seen on Walk 15 from the Digue à la Mer.

A platform for bird-watching is passed on the right. Soon you are driving into a mono-chromatic landscape with no perceptible horizon; the mesmerising silvery-blue **Etang de Vaccarès** shimmers beside you. Most of this vast lagoon (the centre of the region's fishing industry and one of the most important bird habitats) lies within the con-fines of the **Réserve Naturelle**. (Do not confuse the Regional Park, encompassing the whole of the Camargue, with the *inaccessible* Nature Reserve now on your right — indicated on the Michelin map with dotted black lines.)

*In **Villeneuve** (146km) turn right for ETANG DE VACCARES (D36B on maps, C134 on the ground).*

After 2km this narrow road returns to the edge of the lagoon. You can hope to see some of the famous horses and bulls here, and look out on the left for a small thatched house, built to withstand very strong winds — the traditional dwelling of the herdsman or *gardian*. Unmistakeable in their wide-brimmed black felt hats, these 'Camargue cow-boys' astride white horses cut an impressive figure. The head-quarters of the Nature Reserve is located at **La Capellière** (*i*).

*Just past a right-angled bend in the road (Le **Paradis** on Michelin maps, not named on the ground), keep ahead on the C135/D36B at a junction, ignoring the left turn for Salin.*

After 4km you reach the **Digue à la Mer**★, where a sign warns that 4-wheel drive vehicles are prohibited, and *all* traffic is prohibited in wet weather. Continue ahead for 1.2km, to a pumping station, where you can park for Walk 15.

Return towards Le Paradis, but turn right just short of the hamlet on the D36C for SALIN.

You pass the chapel of **St-Bertrand** on the left opposite St-Bertrand farm (cycle rentals, restaurant, B&B).

Some 9km beyond Le Paradis go right on the D36 for SALIN.

Salin-de-Giraud (182km *i*🛒) is the gateway to the salt marshes. Salt has been drawn from the sea here since antiquity; originally destined for the table, today's output is used in the chemical industry. Great piles of salt *(camelles)* stand beside the road, with massive Caterpillars chomping away at them (📷). The tar ends at the 25km-long sweep of the **Plage de Piémanson** (192km). You could continue by car on compacted sand for another 3km, then walk west to the Faraman Lighthouse.

Return past the salt piles and, at the junction with the D36C, keep right on the D36 for ARLES.

This road is very busy; you no longer have the luxury of stopping in your tracks. Fruit trees, conifers, and the fine-leafed tamarisk trees proliferate on the left, but the shimmering rice paddies on the right again

Roman arena at Arles

steal your attention. Pass through **Le Sambuc** and at **Mas de Pontèves** keep right, to continue north on the D36.

When you meet the D570 turn right into ARLES.

There is ample, *free* parking at the railway station in the north of **Arles**★ (240km *i*🏛🛏♿✖ M♨). This city, our favourite of the 'golden triangle' comprising Avignon, Nîmes and Arles, deserves an overnight stay at least. 'Musts' are the Roman arena and theatre, the Espace van Gogh, Place de la République with St-Trophime, and the Alyscamps. *Walk and Eat Around Avignon* describes a walking tour taking in all the main sights, with detailed plan.

From Arles first make for NIMES, but quickly head north on the D15 for BEAUCAIRE.

You pass a large irrigation control station. Vineyards give way to attractive fields of barley, edged by poplar windbreaks.

*From **Beaucaire** retrace your outgoing route back to the **Pont du Gard** (278km).*

Tour 7: LES GARRIGUES

Pont du Gard • Uzès • Anduze • (Grotte des Demoiselles) • Pic St-Loup • St-Martin-de-Londres • Lodève

177km/110mi; about 4-5h driving; Michelin map 339
Walks en route: 7, 16, 17; Walk 8 is neaby
This is a short tour on good roads. There is ample time to see Uzès and the Grotte des Demoiselles, or to walk.
Picnic suggestions: The bubbling Hérault River at **Laroque** (halfway through the tour) makes an attractive setting. Near the end of the tour there is the **Pont de Gignac** (photograph page 44) or, if you have time for a short walk, the ruined hamlet of **Montcalmès** — a gorgeous shady spot. This involves a 4km return detour from Puéchabon: see Short walk 16, page 115.

This tour crosses *the* Garrigues, a limestone plateau stretching from the Gardon to the Hérault and forming a buffer between the mountains to the north and the vineyards of the Mediterranean basin. It's an arid landscape, sun-baked and freckled with holm oaks and aromatic herbs. Suddenly two spectacular peaks erupt off the plain and break the monotony — St-Loup and Hortus. Les Garrigues were traditionally the domain of sheep, and Lodève was an important centre for the wool industry from the 13th century until the mid 1900s.

*Leave **Pont du Gard** by heading west on the D981.*
You pass the picturesque **Château de Castille** and the village of St-Maximin, both on the right. After crossing the **Alzon River** you soon see the towers of **Uzès★** rising ahead.

The town (14km *i✝︎👤✕⚭*) dates from medieval times. A visit is a must; allow two hours *minimum*. Highlights include the 11/16th-century Duché (ducal château), the cathedral, the 12th-century Tour Fenestrelle (the six

storey-high cylindrical bell tower shown overleaf), and the medieval garden.

From Uzès take the D982 west for MOUSSAC and ANDUZE.

An avenue of plane trees welcomes you into pretty **Arpaillargues**, with its old stone houses, flowering balconies, classical church and wrought-iron bell-cage. More planes take you out of Arpaillargues, then you pass Aureillac off to the left. Once in a while a vineyard punctuates the fields of cereal crops lining both sides of the road. After crossing the **river Bourdic** you enter another gorgeous avenue of planes. Just outside **Garrigues** you have a first glimpse of *garrigues*. But the isolated patch of limestone scrubland introduced by this eponymous village quicky ends, and you come back into gentle agricultural land and plane tree avenues.

Just before Moussac, go right on the D18 for BRIGNON, then keep on the D18 for CRUVIERS.

Beyond **Cruviers** the Gardon is seen on the left. Ignore signs to Ners; follow ALES (still D18).

At a T-junction with the D936, turn left for NIMES.

After 2km you cross the **Pont de Ners** (with a lovely view to the right over the Gardon).

Immediately over the bridge, turn hard right on the D982 for ANDUZE, going under the N106.

Crossing a plain, you look ahead to the distant Cévennes.

*Go straight over the D124, D6110 and D24. At the round-about in **Attuech**, take the second exit (D907 for ANDUZE).*

The foothills of the Cévennes are just in front of you. Now cherry orchards take you to **La Madeleine**. From the junction with the D972, there's a view up left to the 12th-century **Château de Tornac** on a hill. Soon the **Gardon d'Anduze** is on your right.
Continue over the railway and follow an avenue of planes into **Anduze** (58km *i🅟🅦*). The village is beautifully sited below high cliffs at the **Porte des Cévennes** — a gorge where two tributaries of the Gardon converge. Take a break in the attractive square, with its classical church and 14th-century clock tower.

Left: the Pont du Gard, one of the most beautiful and impressive monuments in the world, is in almost perfect condition, marred only by the introduction of a road bridge in the 18th century (now closed to vehicles). Completed in the 1st century, the aqueduct carried water from the Eure spring near Uzès to Nîmes — a distance of almost 50km. Where it spans the Gardon, it is the highest watercourse the Romans ever built (49m/160ft). One could sit here all day musing upon the genius of the architects who varied the span and recessing of the arches, to make them both pleasing to the eye and flexible in the event of subsidence. Even the stones protruding from the surface served a dual purpose: they supported scaffolding during restoration work, while at the same time adding visual interest. But ponder too — and with a shudder — the scene at this ancient construction site, with slaves and goats manoeuvering the massive blocks (some weighing as much as six tonnes) into position, then fixing the gigantic clamps used to hold everything together in the absence of mortar. Walk 7 is an ideal way to see the monument from all angles.

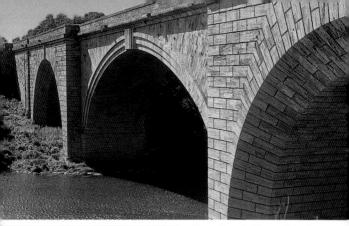

*Above: Pont de Gignac; left: the
Tour Fenestrelle at Uzès*

Leave Anduze on the D133. (It
should be signposted to
ST-HIPPOLYTE, but when we last
checked there was only a small
sign to ST-FELIX-DE-PALLIERES,
with no road number; the road
is to the right of the fountain).

Beyond the 11th-century
Romanesque church in
St-Félix-de-Pallières
(65.5km) you finally come into
Les Garrigues — a scruffy
landscape of holm oaks, acacias
and pines. The road curls down
to the left in front of the clock
tower in **Monoblet** (⌂).

At **St-Hippolyte-du-Fort** follow
CENTRE VILLE and cross the
Vidourle. On coming to a
plane-shaded square, follow
TOUTES DIRECTIONS, to leave on
the D999 for GANGES.

The **Montagne de la Séranne**
stretches out to the left on the
approach to **Ganges** (90km
i⌂). This medieval town was a
silk-weaving centre during the
reign of Louis XIV and still has
a busy textile industry.

Avoid the centre of Ganges by
following TOUTES DIRECTIONS
and then heading south
towards LAROQUE on the D986.

Slanting plane trees take you
into **Laroque** (⌂), where
riverside restaurants line the
Hérault on the right. The river
tumbles over weirs (⌨) and
soon rushes, foaming, into a
dramatic gorge of steep,
orange-hued striated rock.
Kayaks add colour to this
refreshing scene. Further on
there are more kayaking points
at **St-Bauzille-de-Putois**.

(To visit the **Grotte des Demoi-
selles★** watch carefully for the
access road up left: it's 1.6km
beyond 'Canoë le Moulin' at
the start of St-Bauzille; though
it's signposted, still it's easily

missed. These spectacular caves, hide-outs during the Wars of Religion and the Revolution, are best known for the 'Cathedral' and the colossal white stalagmite resembling the Virgin and Child.)

From the **Col de la Cardonille** there is a fine view (⌨🍴) left to a limestone ridge rising straight off the plain and culminating in the Pic St-Loup.

Beyond the col take the first left for N-D DE LONDRES (D1).

Follow *ST-MATTHIEU* and then *TOUTES DIRECTIONS* through flower-filled **Notre-Dame-de-Londres** (♟🍴). You pass the 11th-century church on the right, with the 12th-century chateau behind it, and then the wine co-op on the left. The D1 curls down through oaks to **Pic St-Loup**, then continues east below the mountain. From this angle the stark rusty-hued vertical face of **Hortus**, the mountain on the left, commands attention, while Pic St-Loup tails off on the right.

On coming to a Y-fork where the D1E9 goes left to Valflaunès (117km), turn round and retrace the road. But to park for Walk 17, continue ahead a few kilometres to St-Matthieu (see page 118).

Heading west, St-Loup again dominates the landscape. The ruined **Château de Montferrand** up to the left (Walk 17; photograph pages 118-120) belonged to Raymond VI, but was taken from him during the wars against the Cathars (see panel on page 62).

Some 5km after turning back, go left for MAS DE LONDRES (D122).

The road runs through *garrigues* brightened by a blaze of poppies in spring. Leaving Mas-de-Londres off to the left, the D122 arrives at **St-Martin-de-Londres** (128km ♟🍴). You pass the wine cooperative on the right and catch a glimpse ahead of the clock tower spire. (But to see the lovely 12th-century Romanesque priory church in the arcaded old town you'll have to park and go on foot.)

Turn left at the T-junction where the road ahead is blocked off. Although it is not signed, this is the D32 south.

After 4.5km you pass the turn-off left to the Copper Age **Village Préhistorique de Cambous★** (🏛). Beyond **Viols-le-Fort** you come to **Puéchabon** (143km). (To park for Walk 16, turn right in front of the large calvary at the far end of the village and go right again immediately.) Continue on the D32 through **Aniane**; soon planes lead into **Gignac** (*i*).

In Gignac turn right on the D619 for St-André-de-Sangonis.

The road crosses the Hérault on the **Pont de Gignac★**. Pull up on the right, cross the road *carefully*, and take steps down to admire this lovely 18th-century bridge.

*At **St-André-de-Sangonis** join the A750 motorway for CLERMONT-FERRAND/BEZIERS. Ignore the turn-off for Clermont-l'Hérault and Béziers; keep on the A75 motorway north.*

The environs of **Lodève★** (177km *i*♟🍴) make a convenient touring base. The town is very old: Nero had coins minted here to pay for the upkeep of the Roman legions. The town is dwarfed by the 13th-century St-Fulcran cathedral with its square tower.

Tour 8: CIRQUE DE NAVACELLES

**Lodève • Gorges de l'Hérault • St-Guilhem-le-Désert • Brissac
• Gorges de la Vis • Cirque de Navacelles • Le Caylar • La
Couvertoirade • (detour to the Viaduc de Millau and the
Gorges du Tarn) • Lodève**

*180km/112mi; 7-8h driving;
Michelin map 339*
Walks en route: 18; Walk 16
can be reached by a short
detour, and this route is an
excellent approach to
Montpellier-le-Vieux (Walk
19) and the Gorges du Tarn
(Walks 20 and 21; see detour
route on page 50).
*Some roads are narrow and
winding. The road down to
Navacelles is narrow ('route
difficile' on the Michelin map),
but wide enough for two cars to
pass and built up at the side.*
Picnic suggestions: As you

head north along the **river
Hérault**, you can picnic on
rocks by the Pont du Diable
(30km) or below another
bridge some 25km further
north (opposite the chapel of
St-Etienne-d'Issensac). The
municipal park at **Brissac**
(shown opposite) has shaded
benches. The pools of the **river
Vis** at Navacelles itself are
idyllic, but see also Short walk
18, page 121. Near the end of
the tour, the grassy slopes near
the *lavogne* (paved watering
hole) at **La Couvertoirade** are
pleasant, but offer little shade.

This tour follows the gorgeous green Hérault River
to St-Guilhem-le-Désert with its Romanesque
abbey church. From this exquisite setting we continue
north beside the river and then trace its foaming
tributary, the Vis … to the Cirque de Navacelles — a
landscape so astonishing that you will blink in wonder
and disbelief. Make this a two- or three-day tour and
take in the detour — to the Viaduc de Millau, a man-
made wonder, and the breathtaking Gorges du Tarn.

*From **Lodève** follow MILLAU,
MONTPELLIER. Cross the Pont de
la Bourse and, at the D609
T-junction, go left for MILLAU.
After 0.4km turn right for
SOUMONT, ST-PRIVAT (D153).*

You climb through oaks and
chestnuts, with glimpses of
Lodève below on the right.
Beyond rolling fields of cereals,
the road descends in deep
shade, passing the entrance to
the priory of **St-Michel-de-
Grandmont** (✝) on the right
and then vineyards. Dipping
into a valley, a huddle of
reddish-orange stone houses
appears ahead — **St-Privat**;
Les Salces sits beyond it, on

the far side of the terraced
valley.

*Continue through pretty **Les
Salces**, and after 2km turn left
for ARBORAS (D153E1). At the
D9, turn right for ARBORAS.*

The road descends below the
rocky crown of the **Rocher des
Vierges**, with fine views right
(☞) over a huge tapestry of
vineyards — the Vignoble de
St-Saturnin. Squeeze through
the honey-hued houses of
Arboras; just at the end of the
houses, there's space to pull up
on the right to overlook these
gorgeous vineyards again (☞
and a couple of benches).
*Entering **Montpeyroux** turn*

Park at Brissac

left on the D141ε3 (ST-JEAN-DE-FOS, GIGNAC), then the road bends right in front of the wine co-operative. Just 0.5km further on, bear left for ST-JEAN-DE-FOS (D141).

In **St-Jean-de-Fos** the road becomes the D4.

Keep left for ANIANE and ST-GUILHEM and, just over 1km outside St-Jean turn right on the D27 for ANIANE, GIGNAC.

Immediately after crossing a bridge, turn right and park. There is a fine view to the 11th-century **Pont du Diable★** spanning the Hérault on your right.

Go back over the modern bridge to the D4, then turn right for ST-GUILHEM.

Now following the **Gorges de l'Hérault★**, almost at once you pass the busy **Grotte de Clamouse★** on your left. Soon the river is just beside you on the right, a brilliant emerald green with kayaks whizzing by.

St-Guilhem-le-Désert★ (36km 🚶) lay along the pilgrimage route to Santiago de Compostela (the Chemin de St-Jacques). The 11th-century Romanesque abbey church is magnificent. (Walk 16, which starts only 10km away at Pué-chabon, affords splendid views over St-Guilhem's superb setting below the Cirque de l'Infernet; see photograph page 117.)

The tour continues north on the D4; the gorge has flattened out, but the wide Hérault flows just beside the road (📷). Beyond a weir the road turns away from the river. In the hamlet of **Causse-de-la-Selle** go straight over the round-about on the D4, following

BRISSAC and GANGES. Through the trees you can see the spine of the **Montagne de la Séranne** stretching out on the left. Some 7km beyond Causse-de-la-Selle you pass a 15th-century three-arched humpback bridge on the right; beyond it stands the 15th-century Romanesque church of **St-Etienne-d'Issensac** (🚶). Approaching Brissac, ignore the D108 right to the Grotte des Demoiselles★.

Brissac (62km *i*🚶🏨) has some delightful corners. From the village park (a left turn just past the 12th-century church with its faïence-roofed tower) you have a good view of the 16th-century castle atop the hill. The attractive old kernel of **Cazilhac** is off left, beyond the plane trees.

Just beyond Cazilhac go straight ahead on the D25, following CIRQUE DE NAVACELLES (don't cross the bridge on the right into Ganges).

You leave the Hérault and now skirt the lower **Gorges de la Vis★** from Ganges to Madières. The Vis bounds

47

along on your right, making its presence felt through the very wooded surrounds. Some 2.5km along there is parking and access to a swimming stretch, below a weir. Just past here, a derelict paper mill is passed at **La Papeterie**. As you climb, little hamlets with red tile rooftops keep popping out of hiding. One of them is **Gorniès**, where you cross the Vis. Magnificent conifers introduce **Le Grenouillet** (⊼), and vertical limestone cliffs tower overhead. At a round-about outside **Madières** you have a choice of routes.

You can either go right for ROGUES, NAVACELLES (the northern route to the cirque, with an easier access road) or you can keep to the D25 (ST-MAURICE, NAVACELLES) to approach from the south.

We think the southern route is by far the more dramatic approach. We then *return* via the north and Blandas, to take advantage of the brilliant descent overlooking Madières; this does have the slight disadvantage of repeating the 7km-long stretch between Madières and St-Maurice. Taking the southern route, you pass a small power station just below the road on the right and climb in deep hairpin bends. Just under 5km uphill from Madières, when you are almost at the top of the climb, a large lay-by (📷) on the right affords magnificent views down the gorge. Over to the left is the plateau where you are heading.

At **St-Maurice-Navacelles**

(93km) turn right on the D130 for CIRQUE DE NAVACELLES and BLANDAS.

This road crosses the **Causse du Larzac★**, a limestone plateau peppered with box, *Cistus*, asphodels, honeysuckle and wild flowers. On coming

to a large restaurant, **La Baume Auriol** (98.5km 🖃✕), park and walk to the 'Vue panoramique' behind the building. From here there is a breathtaking view down over the astounding **Cirque de Navacelles**★. It is easy to see why this was one of the hide-outs of the Maquis.

Then continue past the farm, to descend (🖃) to Navacelles. *Take the somewhat vertiginous descent slowly; it's only a short way.* At the T-junction (where Walk 18 leaves the road to follow a path to the source of the Vis), go right into **Navacelles** (102km ▲▲; see also photograph pages 8-9). There is a lovely bridge here, a pretty waterfall, river pools, and a sprinkling of houses.

Return from the village to the junction, and go straight ahead (right) over the river for BLANDAS.

The D713 ascends the canyon, above the Vis (🖃). At a lay-by 2.5km uphill, where you overlook a cedar wood, there is a *Sentier botanique* down to the source of the Vis and the setting shown on pages 122-123 (see lilac line on the map on page 121). Another lay-by under 2km further on offers a fine view back to the *cirque* (🖃).

After leaving the cirque and heading inland, turn right on the D158 for ROGUES.

Under 3km along, just before tiny **Rogues**, look out on your left for the *pink* **Menhir de la Trivalle** and the church of **La Clastre** on the right.

Some 0.3km further on, turn right for MADIERES on the D48.

You pass through the attractive hamlet of **Le Cros**. The road, flanked by oaks, skirts a gorgeous valley on the right (🖃), then descends to superb views over Madières.

*At **Madières** go straight on for ST-MAURICE, crossing the Vis and retracing the gorges. Back*

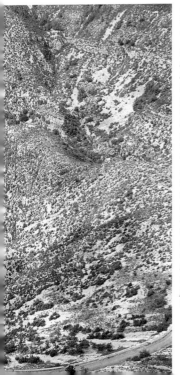

Cirque de Navacelles from the south. Nothing prepares you for this setting: a giant cavity, 300m/1000ft deep, lies beneath you, completely encircled by steep limestone walls. At the bottom sits a hamlet, smoke curling from the chimneys. Beside the hamlet, a 'moat' encircles a tiny hillock. The 'moat' and cirque were created from the original meander of the Vis; then the river cut across the ox-bow to race straight through, a turquoise-blue ribbon tumbling over a waterfall in its haste to escape through a narrow gorge. The overall impression is of a magnificent gem in a flawless setting ... the more so in spring, when the cereal crops in the moat positively shimmer green, like a well-cut emerald caught in strong light.

in St-Maurice (130km) keep ahead for ST-PIERRE. (D25).

This flat road zips straight across a plateau where barley is grown. A wrought-iron cross is passed on the left and then an attractive farm, the Mas-de-Jourdes. (Not far past here you might like to turn left on the D9 and pop in and out of La Vacquerie, just because it is such a pretty hamlet.)

Approaching St-Pierre-de-la-Fage (139km) turn right at the roundabout for LE CAYLAR (D9).

Once more crossing the Causse du Larzac, pull over right some 9km out of St-Pierre (☎), to admire the quilt of fields ahead, each patch edged by tall hedges of white-flowering ash — a magnificent sight in early summer. Not far past here you look ahead to the dolomitic rocks above Le Caylar, where

there is a cross. If you stop at the tourist office in **Le Caylar** (152km *i*☎), notice the carved elm in front. Go straight through this large village with its old houses and clock-tower, following LA PEZADE (D609).

Hugging the motorway, some 2.5km outside Le Caylar, turn right on the D142E5 for NANT and LA COUVERTOIRADE.

The beautifully-preserved 12/14th-century fortified village of **La Couvertoirade★** (159km *i*▮) belonged to the Knights Templar and was refortified by the Hospitaliers. Outside the village walls (a right turn from the main gate) is a fine *lavogne*, suggesting that the knights kept sheep on the *causses*.

Now return to Le Caylar and go south on the A75/E11, back to Lodève (180km) — or head north for the detour below.

DETOUR TO THE VIADUC DE MILLAU AND GORGES DU TARN

Still using Michelin map 339 (or referring to the map in this book), head north on the A75/E11 motorway, soon approaching Millau. You have two choices: you can either cross the new motorway bridge, paying the toll and then leaving at Exit 44 for the Gorges du Tarn, or you can leave the motorway south of Millau (Exit 47) and take the D809 north into the city and on to your base.

Millau is a gateway to the glorious **Gorges du Tarn★**, unfortunately outside the scope of this book. If you plan to do either Walk 20 or 21, we would suggest an overnight stay at **La Malène** (✕☎), about 50km from Exit 44 or 65km from Exit 47 (both routes via the D809, D907, D907b); it's a superb base,

from where you could also take a boat trip along the Tarn.

But if your main priority is to admire the bridge, then spend the night at **Le Rozier** (✕☎), about 30km from Exit 44 (D809, D907). Leave early in the morning, head through Millau and then west on the D992. Just after Creissels, take the *hair-raising* road off left signposted 'Aire de vision du Cap de Coste' — so narrow that you should get there before any traffic is about! A viewpoint near the top allows you to see all the pillars of the **Viaduc de Millau★**, the world's highest road bridge. It is a masterpiece of design and engineering. Le Rozier is also a good base for Walk 19 at **Montpellier-le-Vieux**: take the D29 north.

Tour 9: CASTLES IN THE AIR

Lodève • Cirque de Mourèze • Mons • Olargues • St-Pons-de-Thomières • Mazamet • Carcassonne

184km/114mi; 5-6h driving; Michelin maps 339, 344
Walks en route: 22-28, (29); Walks 19-21 are easily reached from Lodève via Millau, but Walk 21 demands an overnight stay in the Gorges du Tarn. *This short tour leaves plenty of time for you to enjoy one of the superb walks en route — or, if you don't plan to do Car tour 10, to include the Pic de Nore (pick up Car tour 10 at the 138.5km-point). All the roads are good; some are busy.*
Picnic suggestions: At the start of the tour there are five excellent spots. Just short of Octon, you can turn off left to the **Lac du Salagou** (shaded ⊼; overview photograph page 135). At Mérifons you can

drive to the chapel of **St-Pierre** or at La Lieude climb to the **Château de Malavieille** (Short walk 22; photographs page 132) — there are rocks to sit on and shade from the castle walls. **La Mouline** (photograph overleaf), a little further on, is an idyllic setting with ample parking but there is no shade, nor anywhere to perch. In contrast, at the **Cirque de Mourèze** (photograph page 174) you will find plenty of shade and rocks to sit on. About halfway through the tour, the **Gorges d'Héric** (photographs pages 137, 138) make a fantastic setting; see Shorter walk 24-1, page 136, and *allow plenty of time.*

Make for Carcassonne, your base at the end of this long tour through the south of France, and your gateway to the Pyrenees. Lofty castles, all different, provide the focal point. First there is a chance to climb to a ruined 12th-century château and inspect some nearby dinosaur footprints. Not long afterwards you come upon the limestone 'battlements' of the Cirque de Mourèze: while there *is* a real ruined castle here, what captures the imagination are the rock formations, which resemble ruined ramparts. Finally you reach Carcassonne — rising straight up from the plain, the old walled *cité* is a fairy-tale come to life.

*Head south from **Lodève** on the D609 or the A75/E11 and turn off right for LAC DU SALAGOU.*
Where the lake is signed left or right, go right, to skirt the north side of the **Lac du Salagou** (⊼) on the D148. Three high hills jut into the lake, a popular watersports centre, but seem to rise up out of it. Burgundy-red soil enhances this landscape, shown on page 135.
Just before the wine co-op at

Octon (⌂) *take the D148E6 left (MAS DE CLERGUE/MALA VIEILLE). After just 80m, at a Y-fork, keep right (SALASC/MALAVIEILLE). Ignore turnings but, at the next Y-fork (after 200m) go left and immediately left again for SALASC and MERIFONS. At the next Y-fork, 1.6km further on, go right for MERIFONS (D8E3). You enter **Malavieille** after 1.3km. Go straight through.*

Just 0.4km beyond the sign

51

denoting the village exit, you could park for Walk 22. After another 0.5km, stop at the beautifully restored Chapelle St-Pierre at **Mérifons**, shown on page 132.

Meeting the D8 at a T-junction, turn right.

Continue to the hamlet of **La Lieude**. Park on the right below the ruined **Château de Malavieille** (Short walk 22), by a large shelter housing the footprints of prehistoric animals (see notes, page 133).

From here retrace your route back through Malavieille, then turn right for SALASC (D148E11).

Crossing the **river Salagou**, you come upon **La Mouline**, the exquisite setting shown below. The Malavieille château is visible in the northwest.

*At flower-bound **Salasc** (⌂⌂) ignore the D148 left, keep ahead, then go left on the D8 for MOUREZE.*

Soon the **Cirque de Mourèze★** rises on your left, the wonderful 'wild west' setting for Walk 23 (photograph page 174). The French have a perfect word for this chaos of dolomitic rock: *ruiniforme:* the eroded formations resemble ruined monuments, buildings, or even villages. (Walk 19 visits the most famous *ruiniforme* 'village' in the south of France.) Although very touristic, **Mourèze** (28.5km ◼) is beautifully kept.

A ruined castle rises on vertical cliffs above the chaos; the Romanesque church shown on page 135) is much rebuilt. Continue straight through the village. You pass a graveyard for fallen Maquisards on the left.

Turn right on the busy D908.

Soon there is a fine view of the **Montagne de Liausson**, rising behind vineyards. If you did Walk 23, you will know how easy it is — and how rewarding — to climb it.

*Pass to the left of the small industrial town of **Bédarieux**, taking the second exit at the roundabout (D908). At the next roundabout, 3km further on, go straight over (still D908).*

You ignore the first exit, which crosses an attractive modern bridge over the river Orb into Bédarieux. Continue to skirt the river for another 2km.

At the next roundabout take the first exit, the D909A for ST-PONS and HEREPIAN.

You now cross the **river Orb** and drive straight through **Hérépian** (62km).

In the north part of the small town take the third exit from the roundabout, the D908 for LAMALOU and ST-PONS.

Soon you follow a beautiful plane tree avenue for a while. Just beyond the roundabout where the D22 goes right into Lamalou, notice the lovely 12th-century Romanesque

La Mouline

Olargues is dominated by an 11th-century bell tower which crowns the dungeon of its old castle. The castle was taken by Simon de Montfort in 1210 during the crusades against the Cathars (see panel page 62), but only destroyed under Louis XIII.

chapel of **St-Pierre-de-Rhèdes** (✝) in a cemetery on your right.

Some 4km beyond **Le Poujol-sur-Orb** look left for a gorgeous view over the Orb Valley: on sunny days the fair fields and green-gold vineyards of a solitary *domaine* gird the darkly-wooded hillsides like an embroidered belt. In total contrast, the bare peaks of the **Massif du Caroux** soon rise on the right.

Mons-la-Trivalle (77km *i* ⚑), near the confluence of the Jaur and Orb, is the starting point for Walk 24 in the **Gorges d'Héric** — one of the most rewarding walks in the south of France.

A slender 11th-century bell tower welcomes you into beautiful **Olargues★** (⚑). Beyond the railway bridge, you pass a road coming in from Le Cros on the right; Walk 25 descends it. Go through a pretty little gorge and follow the road in a loop to the left, then turn left for OLARGUES CENTRE, to the parking area. There is a fine view to the bell tower and the 12th-century Pont du Diable. Walk 25, a delightful, easy circuit above the village, starts here.

From Olargues you follow the **Jaur** through a very wooded open gorge, passing the large **Aire de St-Vincent** (⛺) on the left, in a basin overlooking the river. **La Canarie** is a large hamlet with lovely stone houses. As you near **Premian**, greenery cloaks the **Espinouse Mountains** ahead of you like a

sable coat. Pretty **Riols**, with its simple Romanesque church, straddles the road.

Bear right on the D612 for MAZAMET and ST-PONS.

There is a roundabout at the Place Forail in **St-Pons-de-Thomières** (100km *i* ✝ ✗ M; see also Car tour 10). Walk 26 begins here, near the superb tourist office. (Walk 29 is also easily approached from St-Pons, via the D907 south.)

Continue west for MAZAMET (D612); refer now to map 344.

Just beyond the D920 left to Carcassonne, you pass the turn-off right to the **Grotte de la Devèze**. From **Labastide-Rouairoux** there is a gorgeous view left to the northern flanks of the **Montagne Noire**, smothered in trees. On the right the **Monts de Lacune** make a pleasant Alpine setting of rolling green hills. Beyond **St-Amans-Soult** (where the first of the churches has an octagonal tower), you approach Mazamet via its industrial outskirts.

At **Mazamet** (135km *i* ✝ M ⚑; see also Car tour 10) you can take a lovely walk, full of history (Walk 27; see pages 146-149).

Leave Mazamet by heading south on the D118.

(Or, if you are not walking, you might like to go to Carcassonne via the **Pic de Nore**. See pages 57-58: follow Car tour 10 from Mazamet.

This adds only 14km, but driving will be slower.)
The D118 climbs past the **Belvédère du Plo de la Bise** (📷 and seasonal *i*), overlooking Mazamet and the colourful old red-roofed factories beside the bounding river **Arnette** (one of the settings for Walk 27; photograph page 149). You pass the D1009 left to the Pic de Nore, then descend through rolling hills and woodlands (🗻). Beyond **Les Martys** you enjoy tantalizing glimpses of the **Dure Valley** on the right — and a wind farm. Chestnut trees line the approach to **Cuxac-Cabardès**, then parcelled-up fields blanket the countryside beyond.
The approach to **Carcassonne** (*i*🕇M⚄) is uninspiring; it betrays nothing of the magic

about to begin. But for a short time the beautiful Canal du Midi (Walk 28; photographs overleaf and page 151) is beside the road.

*Coming into Carcassonne, carefully follow MONTPELLIER and NARBONNE in the one way system, to first circumnavigate and then leave Carcassonne on the N113. Eventually you cross the **Aude** on the Pont Neuf. Take the next right turn for LA CITÉ and assiduously follow signs for LA CITÉ PARKING.*

This signposting takes you to the parking area at **La Cité★** (184km *i*🕇▥✕M; see below), the world's finest example of a medieval fortified town. The *only* way to see it is 'out of hours', so have dinner in the square and then wander the lamp-lit alleyways.

LA CITÉ

La Cité was first fortified by the Romans (1BC) because it lay on the road from the Atlantic to the Mediterranean. Visigoths, Franks, and successive counts carried on the work, until it was interrupted by the wars against the Cathars (see panel page 62), when the town fell

in 15 days. At that time there was only one set of walls (surrounding the Château Comtal, shown in the photograph on page 152), but later in the century Louis IX added an outer wall, beyond the moat. It was then considered impregnable, but history played a cruel trick. Roussillon was annexed, and Carcassonne lost its strategic importance to Perpignan, a town closer to the border. La Cité fell into decay; there was even talk of demolition. But 19th-century Romanticism saw a revival of interest in the Middle Ages; restoration began in 1844 and is ongoing. Notice the slit-holes for archers in the walls and towers, and the wooden gallery, which allowed the defenders to hurl projectiles vertically downwards. Several towers have a projecting 'prow' on the outer side, which helped to deflect incoming projectiles and battering rams.

Tour 10: MONTAGNE NOIRE

Carcassonne • Citou • St-Pons-de-Thomières • Lac de la Raviège • Mazamet • Gorges de l'Arnette • Pic de Nore • Gorges de la Clamoux • Carcassonne

201km/125mi; 6-7h driving; Michelin map 344
Walks en route: 26-28; Walk 29 is also easily reached from St-Pons
All the roads are good, although some are quite narrow. Make sure you have enough petrol before crossing the Montagne Noire whether north- or southbound, and for the circuit of the Lac de la Raviège.

Picnic suggestions: Just under halfway through the tour the **Roc Suzadou** is a fine viewpoint over the Cesse Valley (⊼; little shade). At the end of the tour, there are ⊼ at Trèbes beside the **Canal du Midi**, or you could follow Short walk 28 from Trèbes to picnic in the setting shown overleaf.

The Montagne Noire, the most southerly chain of the Massif Central, is the focal point for this tour. We move from the Minervois vineyards on its parched Mediterranean foothills to lush green highlands and magnificent forests of beech and firs. A brief foray into a more northerly range, the Espinouse, opens our way to the circuit of a lovely man-made lake. Most of the tour lies within the boundaries of the Parc Naturel Régional du Haut-Languedoc, created in 1973 to help these rural communities improve their quality of life, while at the same time preserving the environment and stemming depopulation. (Green tourism is encouraged, with some 2000km of waymarked footpaths in the park.)

Leave **Carcassonne** on the D118 for Mazamet.

You skirt the **Canal du Midi**. (Walkers could be deposited by the roadside to join Walk 28 at the Pont Rouge, where they can cross the bridge to the towpath; see map pages 150-151.)

Just beyond here, take the first exit from the roundabout (D620 for VILLALIER).

You leave the built-up area behind; signs proudly proclaim that you are in the domain of the **Minervois** vineyards and the land of the Cathars (see panel page 62).

Keep right at the junction in **Villalier**, *following VILLEGLY.*

The gentle southern slopes of the **Montagne Noire** rise ahead. The public gardens at **Villegly** are a fine splash of greenery.

At a fork with the D11 bear left for CAUNES; then follow CITOU (still on the D620).

Be sure to turn left on the D620 for CITOU in **Caunes-Minervois** (✇), where the 7th-century Benedictine abbey was restored in the 1700s. (From Caunes you *could* take a circuitous route to Minerve, the village that gave its name to the surrounding area, and the site of one of the most horrific episodes in the Albigensian

Crusade. Walk 29 explores Minerve, but is more easily reached from St-Pons.)

The D620 skirts the wooded gorge of the **Argent-Double** with its rustic stone farmhouses. The Minervois is left behind, and you move from the Mediterranean foothills to the verdant north. The next stretch of the tour, from here to the D612, is the loveliest. Notice the ruins of the château on the hill at **Citou** (31km ⬜) and then the pretty stream falling in tiers on the right. **Lespinassière** is a particularly attractive perched village (⬜🖼). As you climb out of it, stop as soon as you clear the trees: there is a magnificent view back over the village and its restored 15th-century clocktower. Two kilometres further on you pass a sign commemorating Resistance fighters, then enter the **Forêt Domaniale de Nore**.

Beyond the **Col de Salette** you descend to the north flanked by undulating green hills.

At a junction with the D88 to Mazamet, turn right on the D920 for ST-PONS.

Some 3km further on you come to the **Roc Suzadou** (🖼🪑), with a tremendous view over this bucolic countryside — on a clear day!

At a T-junction, go left for VERRIERES (D920).

An avenue of gorgeous chestnut trees takes you through the lovely hamlet of **Aymard**.

At a Y-fork, keep right for ST-PONS (D920).

At **Courniou** (63.5km) you meet the D612. The **Grotte de la Devèze★** is almost opposite, on the road to the station.

The Canal du Midi (Walk 28)

Turn right on the D612.

St-Pons-de-Thomières (68.5km *i*♟✕M♪♫) is the seat of the Regional Park. On approaching the splendid 12th-century cathedral, turn left at the roundabout, to park in the shady Place Forail for Walk 26 or to visit the excellent tourist office. Note that the D612, then D907 south from St-Pons via Rieussec (✕) is the best route to Walk 29 at Minerve.

Leave St-Pons on the D907 north for LA SALVETAT.

Just under 1km after passing the road to Brassac off to the left, keep an eye out on the right for two stone gateposts and a sign, 'La Borio de Roque': you can drop walkers off here for Short walk 26.

You climb into the **Monts de l'Espinouse**. Cross the **Col du Cabaretou**, coming down into fields with conifers and beech

(⌂). After you clear the trees, the hairpin-bend descent offers fine views (📷) down over La Salvetat, at the confluence of the Agout and Vèbre.

Without crossing the bridge to La Salvetat, bear left, then take the second right (LAC DE LA RAVIEGE). Beyond a dairy, go left, again following LAC DE LA RAVIEGE. Cross a bridge and go right (TOUR DU LAC).

You skirt the northern side of the lovely **Lac de la Raviège**, a watersports centre. There is a fine view to the right (📷) over La Salvetat in the valley, below the backdrop of the Espinouse.

*When you meet the D52 turn sharp left for ANGLES, crossing the dam. At a T-junction, go right for ANGLES. Go straight through **Anglès**, following BRASSAC (D68). At the **Col du Fauredon**, go left on the D53 for BOUISSET and MAZAMET.*

Bouisset is a stark village, enlivened only by a bright green well in the centre; in contrast, **Le Rialet** is a pretty red-roofed hamlet. Beyond here you climb into a 'cathedral' of beech and pines.

*Just after passing a small dam on the right at **Le Vintrou**, go right on the D54.*

Descending towards Mazamet, you see the 'Black Mountain' from the most impressive angle: dark granite slopes, clad with firs, rise abruptly from the Thoré plain. Follow CENTRE VILLE into the centre of **Mazamet** (138.5km *i*✝M♒), then follow CARCASSONNE.

Watch for the octagonal tower of St-Sauveur on your left: 400m beyond it, turn left for PRADELLES, PIC DE NORE (D54).

Entering the **Gorges de l'Arnette**, you climb hard by the river, past a series of pictur-

esque stone-built, red-roofed leather works and woollen mills (photograph page 149). The river tumbles down over weirs beside you, and you soon drive past the few houses of **Moulin Maurel**, where Walk 27 begins and ends by the sign for the hamlet.

Some 500m beyond Moulin Maurel turn off left to PIC DE NORE (D87).

Beyond the honey-coloured hamlet of **Les Yés** the mountain views open up. **Tréby** is a forestry house where Black Mountain troups regrouped in June 1944. You climb above beech and firs (**Forêt de Nore**) to a wind-buffeted moonscape, where a rocket-like TV transmitter beckons — the **Pic de Nore★** (1210m/3970ft; 156.5km 🎞). The Espinouse and Lacune massifs rise in the north; in the south the Corbières and Pyrenees are visible.

Turn back from the viewpoint

and, just past the relay station, go left on the D87 for CARCASSONNE.

Ahead, dark conifers pierce the bright canopy of deciduous trees. **Pradelles-Cabardès** is a holiday village in the midst of woods and flower-drenched meadows.

On meeting the D112, go left.

From the watershed of the **Col de la Prade**, you descend in zigzags back into the dry Mediterranean landscape of the **Gorges de la Clamoux**. A solitary patch of vineyards is glimpsed far below — at **Cabrespine** (173.5km 🗒), where a ruined château rises on the right. Attractive cultivation lines the gorge further downhill. A 12th-century tower on the main road at **Villeneuve-Minervois** (◼) mimics Carcassonne with its slate roof.

Keep following CARCASSONNE (D112) until you meet the D620, then turn right and retrace your outgoing route as far as Villalier.

In this flat landscape, the table-topped hill of **Na Aurenque** on your left, with its bib of vineyards, is a pretty picture on the approach to **Villegly**.

*Back in **Villalier**, about 150m past the petrol station on the right, go left on the D101.*

This quiet road, arched with planes, takes you straight to **Trèbes** (✕🛶🍴), where you cross the Canal du Midi (see Short walk 28).

*Now follow CARCASSONNE, taking the D6113 back to the turn-off for **La Cité** (201km).*

This rose window on the north wall of the St-Nazaire Basilica in La Cité is considered the finest in the south of France.

Tour 11: CORBIERES, LAND OF THE CATHARS

Carcassonne • Lagrasse • Château de Quéribus • Duilhac-sous-Peyrepertuse • Gorges de Galamus • Couiza • Limoux • Carcassonne

195km/121mi; about 7h driving; Michelin map 344
Walks en route: 28, 30-34, (35), 36
*There are quite a few narrow roads; the short stretch to the Château de Peyrepertuse (a detour) and the road in the Gorges de Galamus are especially difficult if you meet oncoming traffic. The longest stretch without petrol is between Lagrasse and Rouffiac (72km). If you have time for a **two-day tour**, see Car tour 12: you can head south from the Grau de Maury **towards the Pyrenees**, perhaps breaking your journey within sight of Canigou.*
Picnic suggestions: Early in the tour, at **Termes**, there are two idyllic settings (see Short walks on page 159 and photographs on pages 159-161). Halfway along, at the **Grau de Maury**, a few trees and a stone shelter on the west side of the D123 provide shade, and there is a fine view over to Quéribus. Further along, you can get to the **banks of the Verdouble** by turning right *before* Duilhac (*just past the bridge; see map pages 163-163*). After 2km park at the Moulin de Ribaute picnic area (paid parking in summer). Cross the river on a footbridge (or ford) and walk up the river bed shown on page 164, to the waterfalls. Just beyond **Bugarach**, near the tour's end, you could picnic by the bridge shown on page 172 (see Short walk, page 171).

This tour winds up into the Corbières, last great stronghold of the Cathars. Bounded on the north by the Aude, this upland region rises between the Montagne Noire (Car tour 10) and the Pyrenees. Up until the conquest of Roussillon from Spain, the Corbières were of great strategic importance to France as a bulwark against the kingdom of Aragón. After the fall of the Cathars at Carcassonne, Louis IX fortified La Cité and five more sites in the Corbières — Puilaurens, Peyrepertuse, Quéribus, Termes and Aguilar. These castles, recaptured Albigensian strongholds, became known as the 'five sons of Carcassonne'. With the annexation of Roussillon in 1658 these fortresses lost their strategic importance and fell into ruin, as did Carcassonne.

From **Carcassonne** take the D6113 east. Just as you enter **Trèbes**, turn right on the D3 for LAGRASSE.

Some 5km along, a green basin of vineyards below a hill opens up ahead. A land of *garrigues* interspersed with hard-won vineyards, the **Corbières** yield a rich and fruity wine with a high alcohol content. The vines luxuriate on this calcareous soil; the Romans cultivated the grape in this region.

Beyond **Monze, Pradelles** and **Villemagne** you come into the heavily-wooded **Gorges de l'Alsou** (⊟ with fireplaces).

Vineyards on the D14 between Padern and Cucugnan

On entering **Lagrasse**★ (34km *i✝🛏️✗♻️*; Walk 30, notes pages 156-158) look right as you cross the bridge over the **Orbieu**, to see the 11th-century bridge and 8th-century abbey. Wander the alleys of this gorgeous fortified village, not missing the 13th-century covered market or the highly-decorated 14th-century church.

At the junction 3.5km outside Lagrasse (just past the vineyard shown on page 158), bear right on the D23 for ST-PIERRE, CHATEAU DE TERMES. Then, after 0.65km, turn right on the D212 for ST-PIERRE, CHATEAU DE TERMES.

Beyond **St-Pierre-des-Champs** you follow the sinuous Orbieu through a gorge. A lovely little Romanesque church stands on the right as you skirt honey-hued **St-Martin-des-Puits**. The mountains become more prominent now, and you pass below the ruins of the **Château de Durfort** (🏛️), rising above a meander of the river on the left. This château was abandoned without a fight on the arrival of de Montfort.

Just after circling Durfort, go left for TERMES on the D40.

The **Gorges du Terminet**, a chaos of rock and holly oaks, now lead you to flower-filled **Termes** (55.5km 🏛️; Walk 31; photographs page 159 and overleaf), where the château rises on your right.

From Termes the D40 continues south along a crest between two wooded ravines. The tabletop Montagne de Tauch, with its tower, dominates the landscape to the southeast. Notice the creative topiary of the box hedges at the side of the road.

*At the **Col de Bedos** turn left on the D613 for FELINES.*

Over to the right there is a gentle valley backed by mountains. In spring this stretch is awash with golden broom and white-flowering false acacias.

*Just after entering **Félines**, turn sharp right on the D39 for PALAIRAC, DAVEJEAN, TUCHAN (badly signed). Then go right again on the D139 for*

*DAVEJEAN and MAISONS. In the centre of **Davejean** turn sharp left on the D10 for MAISONS. Climb above Davejean, cross the **Col du Prat** and, at a Y-fork, go left for MAISONS on the D410. At the end of **Maisons** head south on the D123 for MONTGAILLARD and PADERN. Then, less than 2km further on, go sharp left for PADERN (still D123).*

You head straight for the **Montagne de Tauch**. Considering the foothills that have gone before, you're in impressive mountains now. The road skirts the gorges of the **river Torgan** all the way to **Padern** (84km ▢), where another ruined castle on the left dominates the village. After crossing a bridge over the Verdouble, you reach a junction with the D14. (Here you could turn left for a detour through the Fitou vineyards to Tuchan and from there go on to the 13th-century Château d'Aguilar (▮) — or to Ségure, for Walk 35.)

The main tour turns right on the D14, towards CUCUGNAN.

You head southwest along the **Cucugnan Valley** in the setting shown opposite — towards a spike of pale grey rock crowned by the château of Peyrepertuse. The red and honey cluster of **Cucugnan** (*i*), shown on page 167, is up to your right. For Walk 34, park by the *first* road up to the village, where a sign, CENTRE VILLE, points further west along the D14 (for a better road into the centre).

Just past Cucugnan's tourist office, turn sharp left uphill on the D123 for MAURY.

Some 2km uphill, at the **Grau de Maury** ★ (☏), turn left and climb to the parking for the **Château de Quéribus** ★ (93km ▢; see notes for Walk 34 on page 166 and photograph on page 168). From here the whole plain of Roussillon is at your feet, with Canigou rising in the Pyrenees as a centrepiece. Nearby, in the northwest, the silhouette of Peyrepertuse blends so well into a limestone ridge that it is hardly perceptible. On the descent from the castle there is a fine view of the Verdouble and Cucugnan valleys.

*Back at the **Grau de Maury**, turn right, back towards CUCUGNAN. (Or, if you are taking an extra day to see the Pyrenees, turn left and refer to the notes on page 64.) At the junction with the D14 turn left.*

You head west through the most intensively-cultivated stretch on the tour. Vineyards sweep away on both sides of the road, fringed by wooded slopes below white limestone crags.

At the entrance to Duilhac-sous-Peyrepertuse (101km)* keep straight ahead for ROUFFIAC on the D14.

---

*If you are not doing Walk 32, but you wish to visit the 3rd-century **Château de Peyrepertuse** ★, take the *very narrow, vertiginous* road at the entrance to Duilhac *(a detour of 7km return; plus 1h return on foot)*. The largest of the 'sons of Carcassonne', with ramparts over 300m/1000ft long, Peyrepertuse covered an area equal in size to the Cité of Carcassonne! This Cathar stronghold was so inaccessible that even de Montfort dare not lay siege to it. Peyrepertuse was the base for a final attempt to retake Carcassonne (1240); when this failed the castle fell to the royal army without a battle.

The Château de Peyrepertuse, rising above Rouffiac (Walk 32)

LAND OF THE CATHARS
Wherever you drive in this part of southwest France, you will see signposts proudly proclaiming that you are in the land of the Cathars. Catharism, a doctrine of 'purity', took hold in the Languedoc in the early 12th century, in great part as a reaction against the excesses of the church of Rome. Centred on Albi, its adherents (also called **Albi**gensians) fanned out to the south and east, and soon boasted their own bishops and strongholds, including Carcassonne. They counted among their adherents wealthy merchants, artisans and professional people. At this time the Languedoc was in the hands of the Counts Raymond of Toulouse, humanists who tolerated this heretical sect. But the Cathars were a thorn in the side of Rome, and their success led to their eventual downfall. When his envoy was assassinated near St-Gilles (Tour 6) in 1208, Pope Innocent III determined to destroy the heretics. A 'crusade' was mounted. First Béziers fell, then Carcassonne. Although the wars intensified from 1210, under Simon de Montfort's 'scorched earth' policy, only in 1229 was a truce imposed. Even then a few pockets of resistance remained. It took the Inquisition and the burning to death of 200 Cathars at Montségur in 1244 to eradicate the scourge of the 'pure ones'. The kings of France were only too happy to help Rome suppress the sect; they saw the great spoils to be gained. In 1271 Languedoc was officially annexed to France.

Park near the *auberge* (✵) in **Duilhac** for Walk 33; park at the **Col de Grès** 3km past Duilhac for Walk 32. If you need petrol, turn off right into the centre of tiny **Rouffiac-des-Corbières** (⛽), a delightful flower-bound hamlet (where you could also park for Walk 32). Otherwise continue straight ahead (with fine views up left to Peyrepertuse). Notice the attractively coloured stone of the simple church at **Soulatge**. Little parcelled-off gardens hide behind the stone walls at **Cubières-sur-Cinoble** (115km).

In Cubières, turn left on the D10 for ST-PAUL-DE-FENOUILLET.

This *very narrow* road climbs through the **Gorges de Gala-mus★**. Although not very long, its high vertical white rock walls make this one of the most impressive gorges in the eastern Pyrenees. Park 4km along, just before a tunnel. Take the path and long flight of steps down to **St-Antoine-de-Galamus** (✝🏞), for a fine view over the most impressive part of the gorge. (Some 250m past the tunnel there is another parking area with a view to St-Antoine and a seasonal wine-tasting kiosk, but it's a longer walk to the chapel.)

Return to Cubières and turn left on the D14.

The gorgeous village of Termes, on the banks of the Orbieu. Walk 31 is a beautiful circuit, which can include a visit to the château. The building, shown on page 159, fell to de Montfort in 1210 after a siege of four months and was later fortified by St-Louis.

The road now follows the **Agly Valley**, a beautiful swathe of green and gold cultivation. Soon, at the **Col du Linas**, you pass to the right of the **Pech de Bugarach★** (1230m/ 4035ft; Alternative walk 36, photograph page 172), the highest mountain in the Corbières. Beyond the village of **Bugarach** (park near the *mairie* for Walk 36 or 2km further on for Short walk 36), you follow the wooded gorge of the river **Blanque**. It bounds along beside you at **Rennes-les-Bains** (⌂⌂).

Just 3km beyond Rennes turn left on the D613 for COUIZA.

At **Couiza** (151km ▮⌂⌂), there is a well-preserved château and bridge (both 16C).

Go right on the D118 for LIMOUX.

The road bypasses the centre of **Alet-les-Bains** (ruined 11th-century ✝) and comes into **Limoux** (166km *i*✝⌂⌂), known for its carnival and sparkling wine (*blanquette*).

Unless you want to stop in Limoux, well before the town centre, turn right for ST-POLYCARPE and ST-HILAIRE.

You cross the Aude again and can look left to see the old 15th-century bridge and spire of the 13/16th-century Gothic church.

Turn right just over the bridge, then go straight ahead for ST-HILAIRE. Curl left in front of the railway station, then go right for (TOUTES DIRECTIONS).

Keep straight ahead on this road (D104) for PIEUSSE and ST-HILAIRE.

Just under 1km along you pass the Gothic pilgrimage chapel of **Notre-Dame de Marceille** on the left. **Pieusse**, another outpost of the Cathars, is bypassed, and you descend to **St-Hilaire** (✝) in a cradle of vineyards, passing to the right of the Romanesque/Gothic church and 14th-century cloister. It was the Benedictine monks of St-Hilaire who reputedly discovered the secret of *blanquette*. After crossing the river **Lauquet**, the road bypasses the centre of **Verzeille** and comes into **Leuc**.

Outside the village, at a Y-fork, bear right for CAVANAC (D204).

You crest a hill and look down on the plain of Carcassonne.

*Keep straight on, rejoining the D104 and driving under the motorway. At the roundabout, turn right for CAMPING DE LA CITE. Keep to the D104 (one-way system, following LA CITE, then LA CITE PARKING, to arrive at the main gate of **La Cité**, the **Porte Narbonnaise** (195km).*

Tour 12: TOWARDS THE PYRENEES

Château de Quéribus • Castelnou • St-Michel-de-Cuxa • Villefranche-de-Conflent • St-Paul-de-Fenouillet • Couiza

206km/128mi; about 5-6h driving; Michelin map 344
Walks en route: 34 (as a circuit from Quéribus); 36 (if returning via the Gorges de Galamus)
This tour follows many narrow and winding roads; there are also short stretches on the N116 'raceway'.
Picnic suggestions: About two-thirds of the way through the tour, an abandoned farm on the D619 north of Catllar (near the **Pic de Baou**) offers ample shade and rocks to sit on. Some 10km further on, at the **Roman aqueduct at Ansignan**, you could sit on the aqueduct or under it; the arches provide the only shade.

This tour is an ideal companion to Car tour 11 and an excellent gateway to the eastern Pyrenees. If you like what you see, then *Landscapes of the Pyrenees* will take you across the range, to the Atlantic coast.

From the **Grau de Maury** take the D19 south. Leave **Maury** (*i*), with its huge wine cooperatives, on the D117 east for ESTAGEL, PERPIGNAN. In the centre of **Estagel** turn right on the D612 for MILLAS/MONTNER. At the **Col de la Bataille** turn left uphill for Força Réal (D38).

The road is not built up at the edge, but is amply wide and not precipitous. After 4km park below the hermitage (⛪), transmitter mast and steel sculptures of **Forca Réal★**. There is a superb view over the plain and the coast. Inland, Quéribus rises like a needle from the crests and, further west, the Pech de Bugarach can be recognised by its two distinct peaks. As you descend from the hermitage, there is a superb view over the Pyrenees villages south of the N116, with Canigou behind them.

Back at the col, turn left. After 5km turn right at the roundabout and cross the river **Têt**, to enter **Millas** (36.5km). In the centre, turn left on the D916 for PERPIGNAN. But after only 0.6km (just after crossing the river **Boulès**) take the first exit from the roundabout, the D612 for THUIR. After crossing the D16 signposted right for Corbère, take the next main signposted road to the right, the D58 for CAMELAS.

In early summer the peach trees along this road are heavily laden.

View to Canigou from the abandoned farm near the Pic de Baou

St-Michel-de-Cuxa

After 2km take the third exit from the roundabout (D615 for THUIR and CASTELNOU) and at the next roundabout, almost immediately, take the second exit (same signposting).

A narrow road takes you to **Castelnou★**, straddling a knoll in a green basin (*i*⎙). This wonderfully picturesque medieval Catalan village is a beehive of molasses-coloured stone and salmon roofs, surrounded by a bib of vineyards.

Follow CAIXAS to leave Castelnou on the D48.

The summit of Canigou is straight ahead; in the middle distance the chapel of St-Martin rises across the valley, on a mountain to your right. Behind it is the omnipresent Quéribus.

When you meet the D2 at a T-junction, turn sharp right for ST-MICHEL and ILLE S/ TET.

The isolated chapel of **Fontcouverte** (⚐) stands off to the right here in a desolate landscape.
You drop down in hairpin bends to **St-Michel-de-Llotes** and pass below its Romanesque church up to the left.

At a T-junction with the D16, turn left for BOULETERNERE.

Peach, cherry and plum trees line the road to **Bouleternère**, where a Romanesque church rises at the top of the village.

Follow VINÇA and PRADES (D16), then turn left on the N116 for VINÇA and PRADES.

After 4km you pass the **Barrage de Vinça** (⛱), with a Romanesque chapel. The road bypasses Vinça, where there is a lovely Romanesque church tower. After crossing the river

Lentilla you come into **Marquixanes**, where there is another Romanesque church tower on the left. Now, if you have *Landscapes of the Pyrenees* with you and you plan to climb Canigou, either turn left on the D24 for LOS MASOS just over 2km outside Marquixanes or take the fourth exit from the roundabout under 2km further on (D24b for LOS MASOS, VILLERACH).

*Approaching **Prades** (84.5km i), take the third exit from the roundabout (PRADES CENTRE); then, after 2km, turn left for CODALET, TAURINYA (D27).*

This road takes you past the **Abbaye St-Michel-de-Cuxa★** (⚐), where for many years Pablo Casals took charge of the Prades music festival. Canigou rises behind the abbey, its summit snow-capped for much of the year. One of most important religious buildings in the south of France, the 10th-century abbey was founded for the Benedictines. During the Revolution, parts of the building (at that time abandoned) were sold; later a good number of the original columns found their way to the banks of the Hudson River in New York (as did the cloisters of St-Guilhem-le-Désert, visited in Car tour 8). Today the abbey is under the care of Catalonian monks from Montserrat. Set in peach

65

tree orchards, St-Michel almost has the appearance of a *domaine*.

Beyond the attractive 11th-century Romanesque church in **Taurinya**, you come to the **Col de Millères** and pass a *route difficile* which approaches Canigou from the west.

*Just before the centre of **Fillols**, fork right for CORNEILLA (D47).*

Soon the village is visible in the valley, below a high red escarpment. Curl down into **Corneilla-de-Conflent** (⚲) and squeeze between the square tower of the fine 11/12th-century Romanesque church on your right and a round tower on the left. Continue to the beautiful medieval village of **Villefranche-de-Conflent★** (114km *i*⚲☒), and visit the 12th-century church of St-Jacques and the ramparts. First fortified by Spain to confront the 'five sons of Carcassonne', some of the original 11th-century walls remain, but the ramparts are chiefly the work of Vauban (17th century).

*Leave on the N116 for PERPIG-NAN and PRADES. Beyond **Ria**, follow PERPIGNAN and CATLLAR on the Prades ring road, until you can leave it for CATLLAR by taking the second exit at a roundabout (D619). Go through **Catllar**, cross the **Castellane** and, 1km further on, turn sharp right on the D619 for SOURNIA.*

There are magnificent views to Canigou as you climb this narrow road through *garrigues* — the mountain is visible from top to bottom, rising from the plain. Some 10km along you come to a deserted farm on the right, where you can picnic in the setting shown on page 64 (☒), the *only shade* in these sun-drenched *garrigues*. Some 2km past here, at the **Pic de Baou/Col de Roque Jalère** (☒), there is just room to pull over on the right and look north over the huge basin of the Fenouillèdes, with the Corbières range and the Château de Peyrepertuse in the distance. The wedge of the Pech de Bugarach rises to the west of Sournia, which is seen below. Pass the oddly-shaped

The Roman aqueduct over the river Agly at Ansignan

Roc Cornut on the left and keep ahead for SOURNIA. A quarry rises behind unremarkable **Sournia** (128km 🏠).

At the T-junction turn right on the D619 for ST-PAUL. Quickly, at a Y-fork, go right for PEZILLA (D619). After 4km go left for PEZILLA (where the D2 goes right for Ille s/ Têt).

Stone-walled terraces on the left enhance the approach to **Pézilla-de-Conflent**, where a Romanesque tower rises on the left above the red rooftops.

*At a fork 3km beyond Pézilla, keep ahead on the D619 for ANSIGNAN. Over midway through **Ansignan** turn right on the D9 for TRILLA.*

A lovely view over vineyards opens up on the left; they hide a treasure.

Under 1km further on, turn sharp left downhill on a very narrow lane (small signpost, AQUEDUC ROMAIN). Cross a stream, then turn left again.

Soon you see the aqueduct★ (📷) shown opposite, spanning the **Agly** — a gorgeous place to take a break.

*Return to **Ansignan** the same way, then turn right for ST-PAUL (D619).*

The high limestone crags of the most southerly Corbières rise just in front of you as you follow the wooded Agly gorge. Approaching St-Paul, you cross a bridge in a very pretty setting, with the ruins of an old Roman bridge ahead. In **St-Paul-de-Fenouillet** (153km) you have a choice; distances for both routes are approximately the same. Either go north through the GORGES DE GALAMUS★ and pick up Car tour 11 in **Cubières** (the 115km-point), or go via

QUILLAN and join it at **Couiza** (the 151km-point).

*To go via Quillan, turn left in St-Paul on the D117 for FOIX, crossing the Agly. Pass through the outskirts of **Caudiès-de-Fenouillet** and, 6km further on (just after crossing the river **Boulzane**), turn left on the D22 for MONTFORT and PUILAURENS.*

The crenellated silhouette of the château towers above you in a dramatic setting, with the river on the left. In **Puilaurens** turn right on a good road to the **Château de Puilaurens** (□; 45min return on foot). This Cathar stronghold became the 'son of Carcassonne' closest to Aragón.

Return to the D117 and turn left for QUILLAN.

Skirting the river **Aude** (🏕), you bypass Axat, then cross the Aude and follow the narrow **Défilé de Pierre-Lys**, where the river threads through limestone cliffs (🏕). This is a main road used by lorries but, when you can, pull over to look at the rushing river and take in some negative ions. The lovely old part of **Belvianes** is seen off to the right, then the Aude spills over a weir. The wide moss-green river and the plane-shaded road enhance the approach to **Quillan** (194km i🏊). A thriving market and manufacturing town, Quillan is also a good walking base. (From here Cathar devotees can take a detour west on the D117 to the imposing ruins of the Château de Puivert; 32km return.)

*From Quillan take the D118 for CARCASSONNE by keeping straight on where the D117 turns left for Foix. . Still skirting the Aude, you join Car tour 11 at **Couiza** (206km).*

❀ Walking

Those who go to France purely for a walking holiday are likely to be tackling the long linear GR routes. *This book has been written for motorists who want to tour some of the most beautiful roads and enjoy one or two walks en route.* Very few of the walks are strenuous, and we don't include hikes to summits that are easily reached by car (like Ventoux). The walks have been chosen to highlight the great variety of landscapes in western Provence and to focus on our favourite beauty spots.

Although the walks are scattered between Aix and the Pyrenees, you should find many within easy reach (no more than an hour away by car or public transport) wherever you are based. If you are staying in one area for a couple of weeks, visit the nearest tourist office to get information about local walks and up-to-date **bus and train timetables** (some of our walks are accessible by public transport; see 'How to get there' at the top of each walk).

Weather

All the walks in this book may be done the year round, but from mid-June to mid-September it will be far too hot to enjoy any but the easiest rambles. *Moreover, areas prone to forest fires (the Alpilles, Forêt des Cèdres, Dentelles de Montmirail for example) are closed to visitors from mid-July until mid-September*. Spring and autumn are the best walking seasons, with moderate temperatures and an extravaganza of wild flowers and seasonal foliage. On the other hand, you *will* have to put up with a few days of torrential rain. In winter the landscape is more monotone, but the weather is usually dry, clear and cool. The notorious *mistral* blows for about a third of the year (usually in winter and spring and usually for a *minimum* of three days). Often it is difficult to stand upright, and no walks should be attempted in areas exposed to this northerly wind.

What to take

No special equipment is needed for any of the walks, but proper **walking boots** are preferable to any other footwear. Most walks in the south of France cross very stony terrain at some stage, and good ankle support is essential. In wet weather you will also be glad of the waterproofing. A **sunhat** and high-protection **suncream** are equally important; there is a real risk of sunstroke on some walks. Each member of the party should have a small rucksack. *All year round* it is advisable to carry a first-aid kit, whistle, torch, spare socks and bootlaces, and some warm clothing (the *mistral* can blow up suddenly, with temperatures dropping up to 10°C/20°F!). A long-sleeved shirt and long trousers should be worn or carried, both for sun protection and for making your way through the prickly plants of the *maquis*. Depending on the season, you may also need a windproof, lightweight rainwear, woollies and gloves. Optional items include swimwear, a Swiss Army knife, insect repellent and walking stick(s). A mobile phone can be very useful, a smartphone with a simple GPS programme even better, *but* some of the areas in this book still have no coverage. Mineral water is sold almost everywhere in plastic half-litre bottles; *it is imperative that each walker carries at least a half-litre of water — a full litre or more in hot weather.*

Nuisances

We have never been bothered by dogs but, for peace of mind, you might like to invest in an ultrasonic **dog** deterrent: contact Sunflower Books, who sell them. Any snakes you may spot slithering out of your way will probably be harmless, but **vipers** (recognisable by the distinct triangular shape of the head) *do* exist (another good reason always to wear boots and long trousers). Take care if you move a log or stone, and *always* keep a look-out near drystone walls. Outside winter you may be plagued by an encyclopaedic array of **biting insects** — just when you are panting up a mountain or tucking into lunch. You may also encounter **beehives** along some of the routes; bees are not a problem if you keep your distance.

Waymarking, grading, safety

You will encounter **waymarking** on almost all the walks, but this is not necessarily helpful. Many routes have been waymarked over the years with different colours and symbols. Only GR waymarking is meticulously maintained. Local councils change PR routes from year to year, often *without* removing old waymarks.* Moreover, ***our walks do not always follow the waymarked routes***. At the top of each walk we mention the waymarking colours *at time of writing*.

There are three principal types of route:
— **PR ('Petite Randonnée'):** local day walks, waymarked yellow
— **GR ('Grande Randonnée'):** long-distance walks, waymarked red/white (not to be confused with a red flash on a white paint background, which is forestry marking, *not* route marking)
— **GRP ('Grande Randonnée du Pays'):** *recently developed* networks of circular/linear trails of varying lengths, designed to acquaint walkers with a particular region, waymarked red/yellow

Waymarking features common to all three routes:
— A *flash* (stripe of paint) indicates 'Route continues this way';
— A right- or left-angled flash (or an arrow) means 'Change direction';
— An 'X' means 'Wrong way'.

The walks have been **graded** for the deskbound person who nevertheless keeps reasonably fit. Our timings average 4km per hour on the flat, plus a generous 20 minutes for every 100m/300ft of ascent. None of the walks ascends more than about 600m/2000ft. *Do* check your timings against ours on a short walk before tackling one of the longer hikes. Remember, these are *neat walking times;* increase the overall time by *at least one-third* to allow for breaks; *double it* in hot weather!

Safety depends in great part on *knowing what to expect and being properly equipped*. For this reason we urge you to read through the *whole* walk description at your leisure *before* setting out, so that you have a mental picture of each stage of the route and the landmarks. On *most* of our walks you will encounter other people — an advantage if you get into difficulty. Nevertheless, we advise you **never** to walk alone.

Maps
The **maps** in this book have been adapted from IGN 1:25,000 maps but reproduced at a smaller scale of 1:50,000. All the latest IGN maps (the 'Top 25' Series) show many local and long-distance walks. Older IGN maps ('Série Bleue') show *only* GR routes *or none at all*. It is very difficult to plan a short or circular walk using these maps, because they do not indicate permissive routes: 'on the ground' you may come up against

---

*For this reason *never* follow local footpath waymarks without the corresponding *up-to-date* IGN map or details from the tourist office (you may have to buy a book from them). You could find yourself on a dangerous path that has not been maintained for years. Beware, too: any walks described as *'sportif'* are always potentially hazardous!

Walkers in Roussillon's old ochre quarries (Short walk 2)

barbed wire or a new housing estate. If Top 25 maps are not available, seek out up-to-date walks from the local tourist office (see Bibliography on page 6).

Below is a key to the symbols on our walking maps.

═══	motorway	●▶	spring, tank, etc	🚌	bus stop
▬▬▬	main road	∩	aqueduct	🚗	car parking
═══	secondary road	⛪	church.chapel	🚂	railway station
▬▬▬	minor road	†	shrine or cross	🚋	tourist 'train'
─────	motorable track	⊞	cemetery	▮◻	castle, fort.ruins
─────	other track	⊼	picnic tables	▪	specified building
─ ─ ─ ─	cart track, path, trail	⋏	pylon, transmitter	✕∩	quarry, mine.cave
⋯2→	main walk	─⚡─	electricity wires	✶🏛	windmill.stadium
⋯2→	alternative walk	*i*	tourist office	⎸	walkers' signpost
─────	watercourse, pipe	✲	mill	⍓	monument, tower
─ 400 ─	altitude	⍲	rock formation	△	campsite
		▱	best views	⋔	antiquity

Walk 1: COLORADO PROVENÇAL

Distance: 5.5km/3.4mi; 2h30min

Grade: fairly easy, with ascents/descents of about 130m/425ft overall. Good paths and tracks (but some paths can be steep, wet and skiddy); ample shade. Red and white GR, also colour-coded waymarking (see introduction below); *IGN map 3242 OT*

Equipment: see page 68; also mosquito repellent. Refreshments available at two *buvettes*.

How to get there: 🚗 to a car park just south of the D22 (Car tour 1); the turn-off is opposite the D30A to Rustrel. *Paid parking*, with good shade, picnic tables, WC, route map. No convenient 🚌 at time of writing but search www.paca mobilite.fr; English pages)

Short walk: Le Sahara. 2.4km/1.5mi; 1h. Easy. Do 'official' Walk 3 (see introduction). This blue-coded circuit is the best part of the walk.

The whimsically-eroded cliffs, gullies and needles of the Rustrel and Roussillon ochre quarries, once exploited for natural colouring materials, today provide an endless source of fascination for the naturalist and photographer alike. To protect the Colorado's unique landscape (which is in private hands), you are asked to keep to three colour-coded paths detailed in a leaflet you receive when you pay to park. This walk follows 'official' Walk 1, the site's longest route, waymarked orange.

Start out in the CAR PARK: walk southeast on the lane between the Maison du Colorado and the *buvette*. When the lane bends right, go straight ahead on a track (RED/WHITE GR WAYMARKS). Ignore a path off right which is followed in 'official' Walks 2 and 3: you will return that way. For now, your orange arrow, indicating Walk 1, points straight ahead. (Immediately you see how well waymarked this walk is: each route is clearly labelled with large orange, black or blue route numbers and directional arrows printed on white cards and nailed to trees.)
The track narrows to cross the **Dòa** on stepping stones (if the river is too high, you'll have to go back 0.4km to the footbridge shown on the map). It

then broadens out once more and rises quite steeply past a RUINED MILL on the right (**5min**) and then a track off right which cannot be walked

The Sahara

72

without a guide; keep ahead on the GR (☞: *CIRQUE DES BARRIES 1.2KM*). You pass another track that is off bounds and climb again. Then you enjoy your first views into the quarries as you overlook the **Cirque de Barriès** (**25min**), hillocks and eroded 'needles' of sand, called 'fairies' chimneys'.

Some five minutes past this view you come to a fork and *leave the GR* by turning right here on a tunnel-like path through young oaks. As you follow this flat sandy path, fork right at a junction, then descend to cross a stream on logs. Rise up to a T-junction, where you turn left. Quickly,

turn right and descend a sunken path down a stream bed, ignoring narrow side-paths. *Hundreds* of MINI-CAIRNS pop up to guide you on this descent (**40min**).

Go right at another T-junction, where some white cliffs are nearby on the right. At the next T-junction go left, with a stream on your right. After climbing a rather stony path, you find yourself in a sweep of white sand backed by white cliffs and dotted with shady pines, one of which bears the words '**Désert Blanc**' nailed to a tree (**55min**).

Heading over to the right, follow the ☞: *TUNNEL*, dropping

down a steep narrow path to the impressive TUNNEL — 50m long and 10m high. It ends at a balcony viewpoint, so retrace your steps to the Désert Blanc. At a Y-fork, ignore the sign 'Sortie' to the right; go left, to a JUNCTION WITH THE BLACK WALK 2 PATH (**1h05min**). From here it's 15min back to the parking, 1h15min to continue the orange route.

Turn left uphill, soon enjoying a brilliant view over the most impressive **Cheminées de Fées** (Fairies' Chimneys'). Now the path contours for a while, before descending to the right over red soil sprinkled with tiny blue grass lilies. Soon you're at the right of, then *in* a stream bed, sometimes crisscrossing on logs.

You come to a JUNCTION WITH THE BLUE-CODED PATH and a ⏷: CASCADE (**1h50min**), where you could go left to a small waterfall. All three colour-coded paths go right here, making for the **Sahara** (**2h**), the highlight of this walk. You can either follow the orange arrows faithfully, to make a loop to the best vantage points — or you can make straight for the darkest red rocks seen ahead. Then climb the run of red rock on the left, to the top, for the magnificent view shown on pages 72-73 — the highlight of the walk. You're surrounded by an artist's palette of yellows, oranges, mauves and burgundy reds. So intense are these reds, that in bright sunlight the foliage seems to shimmer teal blue!

From the sign ⏷: SAHARA SUITE follow all three routes along a wide sand track. At a signposted junction, *ignore* the path to 'Retour parking' off to the right; keep ahead (⏷: AQUE-DUCT). From the AQUEDUCT (**2h15min**), we briefly *leave* the orange route, just walking ahead on the blue route's outward path and passing a small BUVETTE, La Rinsoulette, with very tasty food. Walk up through the adjacent (defunct and chained off) parking area to the waymarked path just beyond it, and turn right (ARROWS FOR ALL THREE ROUTES). Rejoining your outgoing route, turn left into the PARKING AREA (**2h30min**).

Walk 2: FROM ROUSSILLON TO GORDES

Distance: 9km/5.6mi; 2h20min

Grade: very easy, except for a climb of 150m/500ft at the end. Some stony tracks underfoot; *no shade*. Red and white GR waymarking; *IGN map 3142 OT*

Equipment: see page 68. Refreshments are available at both ends of the walk.

How to get there: 🚌 to Roussillon (Car tours 1 and 2). Return by taxi (rank opposite the château in Gordes), or walk back (Alternative walk). Very infrequent 🚌 line 15-3 serves Roussillon and Gordes from Cavaillon (www.pacamobilite.

fr; the site can be accessed in English).

Short walk: Roussillon's ochre quarries. 30min-1h. Easy. With your back to the TOURIST OFFICE turn right and then left uphill (☞: *SENTIER DES OCHRES*).

Alternative walk: Roussillon — Gordes — Roussillon. 16km/10mi; 4h10min. Grade as main walk. Retrace the GR back to the riding school and the D60, then refer to the lilac lines on the map. Although there is *no* waymarking, the route is easily followed. *Note:* Walk 3 begins and ends in Gordes.

If red is your favourite colour, then this walk will be an eyeful of delight. In spring the rose-tipped leaves of the cherry trees flutter above a carpet of scarlet poppies; in autumn rusty-red leaves mask laden vines. And above these gently-farmed fields rise two magnificently-sited hill villages. The ochre-saturated houses of Roussillon seem to 'grow' out of the quarried hillside; the steeply-stacked, honey-hued buildings of Gordes dominate the plain like an acropolis.

The walk begins on the north side of **Roussillon**, at the junction of the D105 and D169. Follow the D169 towards GORDES. Pass the D102 right to Joucas and Murs (**15min**) but, 200m further on, leave the D169: take a lane on the right (marked as a cul

de sac and with red/white GR 6/97 flashes). There are vine-yards on the left and, beyond them, the villages of Goult, Gordes and Joucas rise from left to right. Beyond a house on the left, keep left at a Y-fork (**25min**). At the next Y-fork (**35min**), keep right. There is

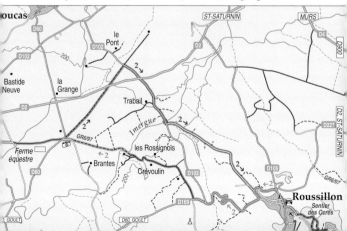

The walk crosses a patchwork quilt of cultivation. Most of the fields are given over to vineyards, and an ingenious machine is used to harvest the crops! But you will also see fields of lavender against a backdrop of the Lubéron (below) and plenty of eye-catching cherry orchards.

another fork just past here, where a track goes left and another half-left to a house. Go half-*right* here, on a footpath/bridleway, crossing the **Imergue Stream** on a concrete footbridge. On the far side of the bridge, at a fork, keep left (red/white flashes). Soon on a cart track, you pass oak tree plantations, as you head straight for Gordes, with the Petit Lubéron stretching out on your left. On reaching the curve of a tarred lane (**50min**) keep straight ahead, towards Gordes.
Cross the D60 and keep straight ahead on a gravel track, passing a riding school

(*Ferme équestre*) on the left. Go straight over a tarred lane (**1h**), now on a tarmac track.
When you come to the D2 (**1h20min**), follow it to the left and cross a bridge over the **Véroncle Stream**. Then, after 200m/yds, turn right on a track (☞: LES GRAILLES, GORGES DE VERONCLE). Gordes is now on the left. At a Y-fork, keep right on the main track. At the next Y-fork (almost immediately), go left uphill (☞: GORDES) and pass through the holiday hamlet of **Les Grailles**, now on tarmac. About eight minutes later, ignore a track up right; keep ahead (slightly downhill) towards Gordes, passing to the right of orchards.
Cross the D102 (**1h35min**) and walk into the farm of **St-Eyriès**. The delightful cart

Above: Gordes, like Roussillon, rises above the plain shown opposite.
Right: the main square at Roussillon, where you can take a break after exploring Roussillon's ochre quarries (below right and page 71) — although smaller, they are every bit as intriguing as those at the Colorado Provençal!

track passes some bories. A tarred lane comes underfoot and takes you to the D2: turn right towards Gordes; the view on the approach is superb. At a Y-fork, go right (↑: GORDES), climbing to the left of a huge house. As you huff and puff uphill, look back across the plain for a fine view of Roussillon. At the next Y-fork, keep right uphill.

Soon a road crosses in front of you: go left downhill. But when this road again curves left downhill, turn right up cobbles. Zigzagging up past cast-iron lamp standards and the old wash-house, this alley (**Rue de la Fontaine**) brings you to the CHATEAU in the centre of **Gordes (2h20min)**, shown on page 80.

Walk 3: GORDES AND THE ABBAYE DE SENANQUE

Distance: 9.5km/6mi; 2h50min

Grade: easy-moderate, with ascents/descents of 300m/1000ft overall. The paths and tracks are fairly stony, and there is little shade en route. *Faded* blue, newer yellow, then red and white GR waymarking; *IGN map 3142 OT*

Equipment: see page 68. Refreshments are available only in Gordes.

How to get there: 🚗 (Car tour 2) or 🚌 to Gordes (line 15-3 serves Gordes from Cavaillon: www.pacamobilite. fr; the site can be accessed in English).

Shorter walk: Gordes — Abbaye de Sénanque — Gordes. 6km/3.7mi; 2h30min. Grade as main walk (ascents/descents of about 250m/820ft overall). Follow the GR6 to the Abbaye de Sénanque and return the same way. Start out in the main square. Facing the Café Provençal (with the CHATEAU behind you), take the D15 signposted to Cavaillon and Sénanque. Pass the FIRE/POLICE STATIONS and BUS STOP, and watch for a FOUNTAIN with non-potable water on your right; turn sharp right uphill on a lane just past the fountain. Beyond a wooden gate on your right, you pick up a red and white GR waymark (5min from the château). On meeting the D177 go right but, after 200m, go left at a Y-fork (GR waymark) When you next meet the D177, at walkers' signposts indicating COTE DE SENANCOLE 460m (a fine viewpoint), continue ahead to another sign, REFUGE A 150M, on your right. On your left a sign indicates a curve in the road: the path down left to the abbey is just by the sign.

NB: The Abbaye de Sénanque (www.senanque.fr) can only be visited on paid guided tours from about 10.00-11.00 (not Sundays or from 12/11-25/01) and from 14.40-16.30; see the website for detailed opening times. The tours are in French, but you can download a guide in English, or get one on the spot. You must be modestly dressed, and you cannot speak or ask questions during the tour — nor can you leave before it is over. The surrounds are freely accessible; the monastery shop is open Mon-Sat 10.00-18.00 (Sun 14.00-18.00); closed most of January.

The magnificent Abbaye de Sénanque, founded by Cistercian monks in the 12th century, is the focal point for this walk. A wonderful feeling of tranquillity pervades the monastery. Pure in line, and lacking in ornamentation, most of the original buildings (and the altar) have survived to this day.

Start out in the MAIN SQUARE at **Gordes**. With the ROUND-ABOUT/WAR MEMORIAL behind you and the CHATEAU on your right, ignore the D15 to Murs straight ahead; take the *next* road to the right, descending just to the left of the POST OFFICE. At a Y-fork, bear right, keeping the drystone walls of the CEMETERY to your left. If you look carefully, you should spot faded BLUE FLASHES on the wall. Beyond the cemetery gate

Above: rows of lavender lead the eye to the Abbaye de Sénanque. Right: Centuries of history unfold at the Village des Bories at Gordes, an outdoor museum of rural life.

The building of bories is believed to date from the Bronze Age, and similar drystone dwellings can be seen as far afield as Ireland, the Balearics, Sardinia and Peru. The bories at Gordes were probably built between the 7th and 15th centuries, but were inhabited until the 18th century.

There is an association in Vaucluse working for the preservation and restoration of drystone structures.

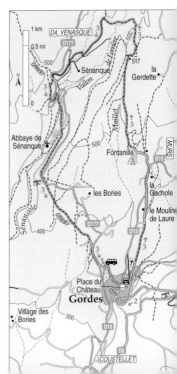

One of their projects was especially fascinating: repairing the 12km-long 'Mur de la Peste', built in the 1720s between Monieux and Cabrières (Car tour 4) to halt the spread of the plague which was racing north from Marseille. At the height of the epidemic, 1000 soldiers manned this drystone wall.

(**5min**), the lane eventually loses its tarred surface. When you come onto tarmac again, by a house, keep straight ahead. Just 120m/yds past here, at a Y-fork, go left, with magnificent drystone walls on either side. Then meet the D15 and go straight ahead for 350m, until you can turn left uphill at a signpost for FONTANILLE and CAMPING DES SOURCES (**25min**). At the next fork, 200m uphill, go left (the lane to the right goes to Fontanille, a large house). After 90m you come to some LETTER-BOXES just before the campsite, where you turn right on a tarmac lane (yellow and blue flashes). After passing a B&B the tarmac runs out and you come to a fork, where a track goes left. Keep

lavender, ignoring the entrance to the farm on your right. The **Sénancole Valley** opens up on the left now. At a fork, where the main yellow-waymarked path goes straight ahead, keep left on a stony track (you may have to walk round a chain) and follow it southwest along the crest. Soon you have glimpses of the abbey, and you can see the Lubéron rising from the distant plain. When you meet a crossing track near the hamlet of **Sénanque** (**1h30min**), turn right downhill. The track curves left and into an open wood, another pleasant, shady picnic spot. Five minutes later you reach a crossroads with several tracks *and no waymarking*. Keep straight ahead here on the level, motorable track. It passes to the right of a pecan grove and a large building (owned by the abbey), and takes you out to the D177 in five minutes. Cross the road, walk left downhill for 30m, then climb a path on the right *(no waymarks)*. In three minutes you meet a crossing path with red and white flashes (GR6/97): turn left downhill. The GR path runs just *above* the drive to the **Abbaye de Sénanque** (**1h50min**) and climbs to the D177 (**2h10min**). Bear right on the road and follow it to walkers' signposts at the **Côte de Sénancole**. Turn right downhill on a stony trail, from where you can see Gordes ahead. When you next meet the D177, follow it for 200m, then fork left down a lane. Meeting the road again, turn left, then curve right, into the centre of **Gordes** (**2h50min**).

straight ahead on a stony path — just a short-cut which rejoins the track. Following the blue and yellow flashes, head due north, rising gently, then descending into the **Vallon de Maillet**. The narrow path runs through *garrigues*, where stunted oaks provide some shade. Clumps of tiny blue May/June-flowering grass lilies *(Aphyllanthes monspeliensis)* dot the path.

After about 1.5km, you come to a T-junction (spot height 517m; **1h05min**). There's a huge pine here, offering good shade for picnicking. Turn right (yellow arrow) but, after 150m/yds, go left down a foot-path (blue and yellow flashes). This wide stony path descends into the **Vallon de Ferrière** — a basin of lavender cultivation. Cross the valley and then climb gently to the left of the

Walk 4: CIRCUIT AROUND BUOUX

Distance: 10km/6.2mi; 2h35min

Grade: fairly easy, with ascents/descents of under 200m/650ft overall on good paths and tracks. Most of the ascents are in full sun. Red/white GR, red/yellow GRP and yellow PR waymarking. IGN map 3242 OT.

Equipment: see page 68. Refreshments available at Séguin and Buoux

How to get there: 🚗 to Séguin. Take the D113 east towards Buoux and turn off after 1.5km for *LES SEGUINS*; park just over 1km along, past the turn-off right to *FORT DE BUOUX* (Car tour 2). No suitable 🚐 at time of writing, but check www.pacamobilite. fr; the site can be accessed in English.

Short walk: Séguin — Deyme — Séguin.
5.5km/3.4mi; 1h25min. Easy, after an initial ascent of 100m/330ft. Follow the main walk for 1h, then turn left on the road (D113). In just over 1km, where the road bends to the right, go left for *LES SEGUINS*; your car is just past the turn-off right to the Fort de Buoux.

A s you approach Séguin, a beautiful limestone edge suddenly appears on your left, on the far side of the Aigue-Brun Valley. This walk takes you along the top of the edge and then to a sunny plateau, before descending back into the valley beneath the slender tower of St-Symphorien and the ruins of the Fort de Buoux.

Start out just west of **Les Séguins**: continue east along the road (now a motorable track) turns left to the **Auberge des Séguins**, head right on a narrow stony track with RED/YELLOW GRP and YELLOW PR WAYMARKS on trees at the left. Rise to a Y-fork with the same waymarks and go left downhill. At a second Y-fork a minute later (*not* waymarked), again go left downhill. Now you have

The extensive ruins of the Fort de Buoux, an oppidum inhabited from the Bronze Age until the reign of Louis XIV

joined the GR9 and you cross the stream (**Aigue-Brun**; **10min**) and then a narrow watercourse.

Soon you're on a beautiful old stone-laid trail that climbs in deep zigzags (make sure, just a few minutes up, that you turn sharp left into the first of these *lacets,* where another path goes straight ahead). At first the climbing edge towers above you on the left. After an easy climb of about 15 minutes you must head up left over bare rock: you'll see GR flashes and the word BUOUX in faded paint on a rock on your left. At the top of this small rise, where SEGUIN is painted on a rock and an arrow points back the way you came, turn left.

Now a lovely earthen path takes you along the TOP OF THE CLIMBING EDGE (**30min**) through holm and holly oaks. A farm (**Marrenon**) is hidden from view above on the right; soon you are skirting its stone walls. Enjoy fine views down left over the Aigue-Brun Valley and, after about 15 minutes, towards the ruined Fort de Buoux almost opposite. When the GR turns off right (by a shed; **45min**), continue *straight ahead* along the cliff-edge (*not* waymarked). Lavender fields sweep away to your right, on the other side of a wall. Soon the path swings north, and the houses of Buoux come into view on the slopes ahead.

The path comes out to a track which is

Climbing above the Auberge des Séguins (top) and farm in the Aigue-Brun Valley (below)

followed to the left in a gentle descent through the hamlet of **Deyme**, where tarmac comes underfoot. We soon join the D113 (**1h**). *The Short walk leaves us here and heads left downhill along this road.*

Take the dirt track straight ahead, passing to the right of the popular **Auberge de la Loube** and cutting a bend off the road. When you reach the road again, turn right and pass to the left of a *gîte d'étape*. Entering **Buoux** (**1h05min**), you'll find a TAP on the right by the village *lavoir* with welcome drinking water. Turn up left on a road just past the tap and just before a TELEPHONE KIOSK. You rejoin the GR9 here; there are WALKERS' SIGNPOSTS on your right. Keep on tarmac, curling round to the left, to pass above a farm and then Buoux CHURCH. Then follow the road in a hairpin bend to the right, passing a SHRINE on the left. Soon, at a CHAPEL, the GR goes right on a track. Head *left* here, through broom, to skirt the chapel on a footpath.

A stony path takes you down into the **Ubac Valley** and to the Renaissance **Château de Buoux** (**1h30min**). At the château turn left on the stony access track and follow it round to left, to a surfaced road. Head straight downhill on this pretty road; tiny fields on the right, shaded by oaks, make pleasant picnic spots. You meet the D113 on a hairpin bend (**1h50min**): turn right. After just under 100m/yds, by WALKERS' SIGNPOSTS, turn left on a motorable track. This forks almost immediately: ahead is a gate to Mas Aigue Brun. Turn left on the *footpath* just in front of the gate (there

is a handwritten ☞: 'BUOUX, SEGUINS, FORT'). You descend in deep shade and can hear the stream close by.

Ignoring tracks off left, then right, you cross the **Aigue Brun** on a beautiful LOG FOOTBRIDGE (**2h**) and rise to the U-bend of a track with a letterbox. Head right (handwritten ☞: BUOUX LE FORT). Five minutes *take care:* turn up sharp left on another track; *do not* go straight on. This track quickly narrows to a path; you can hear the river below and see over to the climbing wall you tackled at the start of the walk.

Coming to a Y-fork, go right (the fork to the left is private property, usually chained off). Your path rises almost imperceptibly and, looking behind you, you should be able to see the tower of **St-Symphorien** peeping above the greenery. When we first saw this lovely 10th century priory it was in ruins, but in the early 21st century it was bought (from the film director Roger Vadim's family) and restored as a private home.

Eventually the path descends and brings you back down to the banks of the stream, where you pass a grassy area on the left with a couple of derelict picnic tables. Meeting the road (**2h25min**), head right. If you're here on a weekend, you will be treated to the breath-taking spectacle of climbers swarming over the edge like flies on a honey-pot. If you haven't already visited the **Fort de Buoux**, do so now (allow 1h extra). Or make for aptly-named 'Needle Rock' (**L'Aiguille**); it rises just beyond your PARKING PLACE (**2h35min**).

Walk 5: FORET DES CEDRES

Distance: 7.5km/4.7mi; 2h25min
Grade: easy; descent/ascent of 100m/330ft; some stony paths and tracks. Ample shade. Yellow, and *faint* blue waymarking; some cairns. *IGN map 3142 OT*

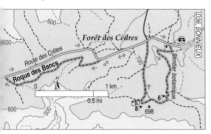

NB: See notes on page 68 about summer closure of some walks.
Equipment: see page 68; nearest refreshments at Bonnieux
How to get there: 🚌 to the Forêt des Cèdres, signposted off the D36 (1.5km south of Bonnieux). Paid parking at the vehicle barriers (Car tours 2, 4). No 🚐 service.

Short walks
1 Sentier botanique. 3km/2mi; 1h08min. Grade as above. Follow the main walk for 1h05min, then return along the road to your car.

2 Roque des Bancs. 5km/3mi; 1h25min. Easy, level walking. Walk west along the Route des Crêtes for 15 minutes, until you come to a water tank on your left. Then pick up the main walk at the 1h15min-point.

3 Viewpoint. 2km/1mi; 30min. Very easy. Follow the main walk *past* the *Sentier botanique* sign; then, 250m/yds further on, turn left on a wide path, to a fine viewpoint by 🔭 8. Return the same way.

Cedars from the Atlas Mountains of northern Africa were introduced on the heights of the Petit Lubéron in the mid 1800s. The trees flourished — as did the insects and mushrooms which arrived with them. A nature trail *(Sentier botanique)* with information panels tells you more about the wealth of flora and fauna on the massif.

Start out at the PARKING AREA: follow the road behind the barrier preventing vehicle access to the **Route des Crêtes**, the narrow tarmac road on the crest of the **Petit Lubéron**. After 150m/yds turn left (🔭: SENTIER BOTANIQUE, yellow waymarking). Descend gently through cedars and then *garrigues*. In spring watch out for pockets of bright-white star-of-Bethlehem (*Ornithogalum umbellatum*) and the slender stalks of the rock sainfoin (*Hedysarum saxatile*), capped by a pyramid of pale pink florets. At the BOTTOM OF THE VALLEY (**30min**), where holm oak from these slopes used to be smouldered into charcoal, go right uphill at the fork. This stony path forks five minutes later: go either way. The two paths quickly rejoin at a WAYMARKING PEG, where you come to another fork: go left uphill. In two minutes, at a T-junction, go right, passing 🔭6. At the next fork, seven minutes later, climb left uphill to a plateau. This ancient pastureland is no longer grazed and has been invaded by box,

*Above: The Route des Crêtes is
closed to traffic for the enjoyment of
walkers. Right: caves cut into the
Roc des Bancs have been used as
hideouts for centuries, most recently
by the Maquis.*

like so many other upland areas
we visit. At ⌐8 (**55min**) you
come to a splendid VIEWPOINT
over the Durance Valley, with
the Montagne Ste-Victoire
visible to the left and the
Alpilles to the far right.
From here head north on a
stony track, to rejoin the
Route des Crêtes in 10
minutes. Turn left and follow it
to WATER TANK 41 (**1h15min**).
Head left here, on a footpath
(there was *faint blue* waymarking the last time we
checked this walk) and ignore a
path off to the right almost at
once. When you come to a fork
in about seven minutes, turn
right (ARROW). Now a shady
path lined with wild flowers
and junipers takes you below a
limestone edge (**Roc des
Bancs**), past the odd small cave
and, eventually, to a BERGERIE
beneath a rock overhang

(**1h40min**). Three minutes
past this shepherds' shelter go
right at a fork. The path is ill-
defined at this point, but just
head northwest, keeping an eye
out for CAIRNS. Ten minutes
later, turn right on the **Route
des Crêtes** and follow it 30
minutes, back to the CAR PARK
(**2h25min**).

85

Walk 6: DENTELLES DE MONTMIRAIL

Distance: 8km/5mi; 3h25min
Grade: moderate-strenuous, with ascents/descents of 350m/1150ft overall. Some of the descent paths are steep and stony; you must be sure-footed and agile, but the paths are not vertiginous. Adequate shade. Blue, then yellow PR waymarking. *IGN map 3040 ET NB: See notes on page 68 about summer closure of some walks.*
Equipment: see page 68; walking stick(s). No refreshments available beyond Gigondas
How to get there: 🚗 to the Col du Cayron (large parking area). From Gigondas (Car tour 3) follow LES FLORETS, DENTELLES DE MONTMIRAIL. When the road reverts to track continue ahead for another 0.7km and park at the col, just

over 2km from the turn-off. There is a 🚐 (Line J) to Gigondas from Carpentras, but it is for schoolchildren and not convenient (see www.trans-comtat.fr *or* www.pacamobi lite.fr). To walk to the Col du Cayron from Gigondas add 4km/1h15min return).
Short walk: Col du Cayron — Rocher du Midi — Col du Cayron. 3.5km/2.2mi; 1h40min. Moderate climb/descent of 220m/720ft, *requiring agility.* Follow the main walk to the crest, then return to the T-junction at the 25min-point and head left. The path climbs a bit initially, then leaves the crest and after 30 minutes descends to the Rocher du Midi (🍴). There turn right on the track back to the col.

One of the most exquisite walks you will ever take, *anywhere,* this magnificent hike leads you up, over and between the Dentelles and their glistening vineyards — with splendid views to Mont Ventoux.

Start out at the **Col du Cayron** (394m): first follow the yellow walkers' ⌐: COL D'ALSAU 2,5KM, then climb the signposted SENTIER D'ACCES AUX DENTELLES. From here until you reach the Col d'Alsau, *carefully follow* the blue dots. At a T-junction (**25min**), where both directions are waymarked in blue, keep left uphill; the path to the right is followed in the Short walk. Six minutes later you are in the setting shown opposite (above). *(The Short walk returns to the T-junction from here.)*
Turn right and scramble along the undulating ridge, rounding the **Rocher du Turc** with its 'window' (626m/2050ft, the highest point in the Dentelles).

If you spot it, ignore a path heading back sharp left to the Rocher du Turc (**1h**); it is reputedly very difficult, and we have not done it. Instead, keep ahead beneath the 'window' of the **Tête Vieille.** Soon the steep descent begins (sometimes on all fours); this drops you down to the pine-scented **Col d'Alsau** (445m; **1h15min**).
Turn left at the col but, after 100m/yds, turn left uphill on an equally wide track (⌐: CANTON DU CLAPIS, ignoring the track right to Beaumes-de-Venise. At a Y-fork almost immediately, climb steps to the right (blue *and yellow waymarks*). The climb quickly levels out, as you skirt the **Grand Montmirail**

86

You climb quickly to the ridge atop the Dentelles Sarrasines (top and right), where you follow the path west past a stupendous array of jagged rocks pierced with 'windows'.

on your right. *Now you must **assiduously** follow sparse **but crucial yellow** waymarks.* Make for the 'needle' of rock eventually seen ahead in the valley (the western edge of the **Lame du Clapis**). Just as you reach the 'needle' (blue dot), skirt to the left of it and then scramble up over bedrock (faded blue dot and faded arrow pointing back in the direction from which you've come).

Beyond here, bear in mind that you must cross to the far side of the valley *before* it becomes a gorge. Watch for the *yellow*

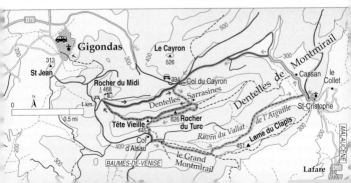

From the Chapelle St-Christophe, there is a fine view west over vineyards to Mont Ventoux.

waymarks and, when the path forks, keep to the lower path. This takes you *very steeply* down to the left in hairpins, where you cross the pretty rock pools of the **Ravin du Vallat de l'Aiguille (2h)**. Just past here, at a three-way fork, keep straight ahead.

Soon the pine-scented path heads east towards a 'sugar loaf' hill. Cross two streams; beyond the second keep straight ahead, with a vineyard on your left *(no waymarks)*. Rise up to a lane **(2h25min)**. Turn right and, at a bend, climb the path up left to the beautifully-sited **Chapelle St-Christophe (2h35min)**, a shady spot for a break. Then return to the lane and turn right. Some 450m/yds beyond **Cassan**, at a fork **(2h50min)**, go left past vineyards, back to the **Col du Cayron (3h25min)**.

Walk 7: PONT DU GARD

See also photograph page 42
Distance: 7km/4.3mi; 2h10min
Grade: easy, with ascents/descents of little more than 100m/330ft overall. Some agility needed on the 'Panorama' path. Avoid weekends and holidays, when the site is swarming with people. Yellow PR and some red and white GR waymarking. Limited shade. *IGN map 2941 OT Note:* If car are racing at the nearby circuit, the whole experience will be marred.
Equipment: see page 68; swimming things; refreshments available at Vers and the Pont du Gard

How to get there: 🚗 to Vers-Pont-du-Gard (a detour on Car tour 4). Vers is north of the D981 between Uzès and Pont du Gard (Rive Gauche). Park at the Place de la Fontaine. Or 🚌 to Vers (line 205 from Avignon or line 168 from Nîmes: www.stdgard.com/accueil.htm). Note that most buses stop at the wine co-op south of the centre, but the 11.00 bus from Nîmes stops at the Place de la Fontaine (also called 'Les Platanes', for the many plane trees surrounding the fountain). This is where we

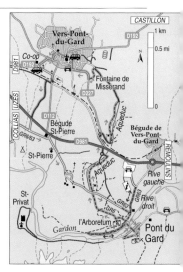

start; if you alight at the wine co-op, pick up the notes after the 5min-point.
Short walk: Rive Droite and Rive Gauche. 2.5km/1.6mi; 1h. Grade as main walk. 🚗 to the huge car park at Rive Gauche. Walk to the bridge, then follow the main walk from the 50min-point to the 1h20min-point. Then walk back down to the river and follow the nature trail for as long as you like, before returning to the car park.
Alternative walk: see Walk 8

Now a UNESCO World Heritage site, the Pont du Gard is a colossal work of art, to be admired from all angles, and in different lights. Plan to devote a full day to this beautiful and varied five-star walk, taking a long break on the banks of the Gardon and spending some time at the fascinating visitors' centre.

Start out in **Vers**, at the **Place de la Fontaine** (where there is a bus stop called LES PLATANES). Follow the road signposted to Uzès, passing to the right of the CHURCH and going along **Avenue d'Alba**

and then **Rue des Ecoles**. At the SCHOOL (on your right), turn left on **Rue de Palezieux**. After the road bends right (still the D192, signposted to Uzès), take the first sealed left turn; on your left is the **Lavoir**

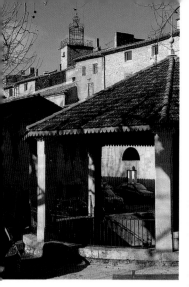

We begin the walk here at the Place de la Fontaine in Vers — 'fontaine' refers to this old wash-house (lavoir) in the centre of the square. Note the charming wrought-iron bell-cage on the church in the background.

de Font d'Izière (**5min**; *YELLOW WAYMARKS*). Coming to a T-junction, with the *WINE CO-OPERATIVE* on your right, turn *left* towards *REMOULINS*, passing an *IRON CRUCIFIX* on the left. (If you came by bus, the wine co-op is where you will catch the return bus, even if you arrived at Les Platanes.) At another T-junction, turn right in front of the *CEMETERY*. Cross the *RAILWAY*, then immediately turn right and, after 100m/yds, turn left on a cart track through vineyards, cherry orchards and olive groves.

Cross the D981 and continue straight ahead (almost directly opposite) on a tarred lane towards *LA BÉGUDE ST-PIERRE*. Then turn left on **Chemin du Passeur**, joining the **GR6/63**. As you pass the **Hotel La Bégude St-Pierre**, turn right just in front of its car park and continue on a lane. On the right, the ruined **Chapelle St-Pierre** (**30min**), sits in a field of golden cereals and poppies, with poppies sprouting from its roof.

Ignore a track to the left just

past the chapel and any other trails off left or right. Coming to a T-junction, follow the lane to the left round a *METAL BARRIER*, quickly passing a house on the right.

When you reach a barrage of *SIGNPOSTS* (**45min**), keep to the lane along the GR63 (☛: *PONT DU GARD 0,9KM*). ('Pont du Gard' *should* also be signposted half-right here via the GR6. The sign was missing when we checked just before press date, but the GR6 is our return route.)

When the tarmac ends, descend ahead to a walkway (**50min**): the **Pont du Gard** is to your right. Follow the paved path and cross the bridge. On the far side, take steps up to the right, to a fine view of the river and bridge. At the top of the steps, turn right for *PANORAMA* (**55min**), following GR waymarks. Beyond the *VIEWPOINT* (just a couple of minutes up), continue on this path which zigzags back down to the river.

Meeting the lane on the south side of the bridge, turn right, walk below one of the arches and after 100m/yds, turn back sharp right to cross back to the *rive gauche* (left bank). From here you could explore the arboretum just above the river for as long as you like. But the main walk goes straight ahead up steps (☛: *GR6/63, PR41*). From here on, the maze of paths through the *garrigues* can be confusing, so keep a close eye on the yellow and red and

The mighty span of the pont du Gard: see it from all angles!

white waymarks; *you should always be on a strong, clear, waymarked path.* But first make a short detour left, to the left bank's PANORAMA (**1h20min**). The route goes through a beautiful wood of holly and holm oak, where the yellow and red fruits of the strawberry tree and pink *Cistus* shine against the dark foliage. Soon remains of the old aqueduct begin appearing on the left. When you come back to the SIGNPOSTS first encountered at the 45min-point (**1h30min**), cross straight over the lane (☞: VERS). There are even more substantial remains on this stretch. At a crossing with a lane on the left and a track to the right, go straight ahead up a steep dirt path. There is a beautiful setting not far along, with rocks placed in a circle beneath a huge holm oak on the right — a perfect picnic spot.

Soon steps take you down an embankment, to a track just above the D981. Walk 100m/yds to the left on the track, to a small roundabout. Go right, cross the D981 *carefully,* then go straight ahead on a road signposted CARRIERES DE VERS-EST. Cross the RAILWAY (**1h50min**) and immediately turn right up a motorable gravel track. At the top of the rise, make a U-turn to the left (☞: FONTAINE MENESTIERE), then keep left at a Y-fork. The arches and buttresses of the ruined aqueduct are still beside you.

Keep left at two more Y-forks and then turn left at a T-junction; *watch the yellow waymarks on this stretch!* Finally the aqueduct ends and you come onto a motorable track: keep straight ahead. Just as this track becomes tarred (by a FIRE HYDRANT on the left), turn left on a pretty woodland path. It comes down to the D227 at the **Fontaine de Misserand**. Turn right on the road, then take the first right uphill (RUE DU LAVOIR). Keep straight ahead past any turn-offs. At a T-junction go left downhill (**Chemin des Crozes**). Continue to the **Place de la Fontaine** (**2h20min**). If you came by bus, remember that all buses *depart* from the wine co-op, so pick up the walk from the start and make your way there.

But first take a look around Vers or have a drink at the bar in the church square. The tourist office has an interesting website (www.ot-pontdugard. com): the site can be accessed in English and has more ideas for walks in the area.

91

Walk 8: GORGES DU GARDON

Distance: 11km/6.8mi; 3h05min

Grade: easy, level walking, but the bedrock sections can be very slippery when wet. The short, steep ascent to the Chapelle St-Vérédème demands a head for heights. Yellow PR waymarks. *IGN map 2941 OT*

Equipment: see page 68; optional bathing things; *strong torch* mandatory, if you want to explore the Grotte de la Baume, a cave/tunnel. Refrements available at Collias

How to get there: 🚗 to Collias (Car tour 5); park at the FOYER CULTUREL on the D3 in the village. Collias is served by 🚌 line 168 from Nîmes (www.stdgard.com/accueil.htm).

Alternative walks

1 Return via Les Condamines. 12.5km/7.8mi; 4h15min. Moderate, with ascents/descents of about 150m/490ft, requiring agility. Virtually *no shade*. If you want to make the walk circular, return to the 1h20min-point and climb the steep path and then a *very* steep escarpment (*RED DOTS, YELLOW FLASHES*). Beyond a vineyard on the right, you meet a cart track (40min). Turn left and, after 25m/yds, at the **Les Condamines** signpost, follow ⌖: COLLIAS 5.7KM. 300m/yds further on, at a Y-fork, ignore signposting left to Collias; keep *right* following *sparse* GR waymarks (⌖: MENUDE; GR6/63). This stony track leads back to Collias. The views north over the Alzon Valley are fine (and you can also divert right to some viewpoints over the Gardon), but in heat the route is soul-destroying.

2 Collias — Pont du Gard. (6.5km/4mi; 2h15min). This walk is part of a network of hikes in the Gardon. You could, for instance, link up with Walk 7. A good route map for the Gardon, showing signposting as well, is usually available from the local tourist offices.

This splendid walk is best reserved for a quiet week-day out of season, to ensure absolute tranquillity. The hundreds of caves along the little gorge were inhabited in paleolithic times; today much of the riverbank is a nature reserve, where fish and beavers thrive. The once-cultivated fields are overgrown with wild flowers, a magnet for butterflies.

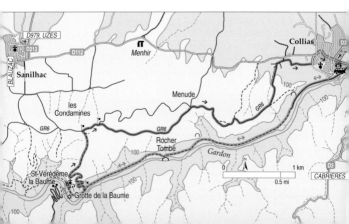

View over the Gardon from the Chapelle St-Vérédème

Start out at the FOYER CULTUREL in **Collias**: walk south to the river and descend the steps just before the bridge (⊪: LA BAUME). At the bottom of the steps, take the road ahead and continue on track past a kayaking centre. Beyond a restaurant, you're on a wide shady track beside the **Gardon**. Rock walls rise on your right, while the far bank is backed by gentle wooded hills. Soon the way narrows to a riverside path. You *may* come to a point (after about **20min**) where the path has been diverted away from the river for a short

93

The watermill and old dam at La Baume; the dam fell victim to storms in 2002 and has not been rebuilt.

stretch to protect the beavers' habitat; if so, *watch out* for the tree stumps in the path.)

After passing a nature reserve sign asking you to keep to the main path, you come to the most beautiful stretch, as you continue over bedrock. The river is utterly placid, limpid, and brimming with surprisingly large fish. Then the path moves inland through tall golden grasses full of wild flowers, where legumes and sugar cane testify to cultivation in centuries past.

Some rapids are passed and the path crosses a short ledge below a huge boulder, the **Rocher Tombé (45min)** before running alongside the river again. Notice the pink and white marble-like bedrock underfoot.

Finally you come to another signpost indicating a path climbing to the right (◀: LES CONDAMINES; **1h20min**). *(This is the easiest ascent for the Alternative walk.)* Ahead are the ruins of **La Baume** on the far bank. Unless you have a head for heights, this is a good

94

place to end the walk with a picnic, while you watch the kayakers.

The main walk continues past a WATERMILL (**1h25min**), turns north and then zigzags uphill (partially on steps) to the ruined **Chapelle St-Vérédème** (**1h35min**). A monk's cell is to the left of the chapel and a narrow, exposed, cliff-edge path runs to the right of it. Follow this short path through an iron gate, to **La Baume**, an enormous cave-tunnel. *Don't go more than a few steps into this cave/tunnel unless you have a very good torch;* it is enormous, pitch black (because it curves), and can be extremely frightening. On the other hand, if you *do* have a good torch and you are keen to do Alternative walk 1, you can walk *through* this cave/tunnel and then follow a short path which leads to the steep Condamines ascent.

The best way to end the walk is to retrace your steps along the riverbank to **Collias** (**3h05min**).

Walk 9: CIRCUIT TO THE CASCADES DU SAUTADET

Distance: 6.5km/4mi; 2h30min

Grade: quite easy, with an ascent/descent of 175m/575ft. The initial ascent is on a lane and stony track in full sun, but then shady paths come underfoot. There may be boar-shooting in the woods above La Roque in autumn (usually on Wed/Sat/Sun). *No way-marking. IGN map 2940 OT*

Equipment: see page 68; bathing things. Refreshments available at La Roque

How to get there: 🚗 to La Roque-sur-Cèze (optional detour on Car tours 4, 5, 6). From Remoulins take the D6086 north. Just past Bagnols-sur-Cèze, turn left on the D980 for BARJAC and after about 9km turn left again for LA ROQUE. Cross the old bridge (one-way system; traffic light) and turn down right into the large shaded parking area. No suitable bus at time of writing,

but check at the nearest tourist office or at www.stdgard. com/accueil.htm.

Short walk/picnic suggestion: Cascades du Sautadet. 40min. Easy. From the car park, follow the lane on the west side of the river to the waterfalls and back.

This woodland walk, with an optional swim at the end, is ideal for a warm day. Much of the route is in deep shade, on leaf-soft, sunken footpaths, before emerging in vineyards. The 13th-century arched bridge at La Roque is a beauty, and the village worth a visit. But without doubt it is the splendid maze of waterfalls the Cèze has cut into the limestone rock at the Cascades du Sautadet that will stay in your memory.

Start the walk at the PARKING AREA below **La Roque**: follow the road up into the village. Curl left uphill in front of the CHURCH on the **Grande Rue**, pass a tiny square on the left, and then keep straight ahead up a stone-laid road (still the **Grande Rue**). Pass the **Mairie** on the left (**9min**), then head left above it on the **Chemin de Bellefeuille**, passing a few

Old bridge at La Roque

houses. At a three-way fork (where the tar runs out; **15min**), take the middle track. Six minutes later, ignore a track off left. Two minutes further on, you come to a Y-fork of tracks. Turn left here, immediately passing a vineyard on the right and enjoying a pleasant view northwest over the Cèze Valley. One minute after passing a vineyard on the left, at a Y-fork, keep left, passing a lean-to and hunters' barbecue (for wild boar) on the left immediately.

The way continues through a thick *maquis* of junipers, holm oaks, strawberry trees, pines, and bright pink-flowering *Cistus*. Soon bedrock comes underfoot — an especially attractive section.

Beyond a rise (**50min**), a lovely woodland trail with moss underfoot undulates to the CREST of the **Rochers de Descattes** (**55min**). Here the main trail turns 90° left, but you must *turn off right* on a strong path. (The main trail continues along the crest, with fine views after 10-15 minutes.) Just 5m/yds downhill, your path curls left and you can see a LARGE CAIRN

Cascades du Sautadet: Legend has it that Hannibal's daughter drowned here, while trying to cross the river on her elephant…

La Roque: in this part of Provence rose bushes are often planted at the ends of rows of vines.

just below. Beyond the cairn, the path (sometimes sunken) descends gently southeast through a dense canopy of oaks.

When you come to a clearing with a HUGE DEAD OAK in the centre, ignore the track ahead. Turn 90° left on a level path, also sunken, through shady mixed woodland. You may spot some holes underfoot, where wild boar have been rooting. Ignore all side paths as you traverse east, eventually through a patch of maritime pines.

The path emerges on a track in front of a VINEYARD (**1h30min**), with a fine view across the Cèze Valley and back up to the Rochers de Descattes. Follow this cart track to the right and descend straight ahead between vineyards, ignoring tracks left and right. You pass a farm on the left (perhaps with *unchained*

dogs) and immediately come to the D166. Opposite is a lane to a camp site, but take the track just at the left of this lane. At the Y-fork which comes up in a minute, go left downhill on a rocky path (ignoring a track which comes in from the right). Three minutes later, at a T-junction with a track, turn left downhill (a gated entrance is to the right). Ignore a track coming in from the left behind you four minutes later. Two minutes after that, join a lane and keep left, between oaks on the left and and vineyards and acacias on the right.

Just 10m/yds *before* joining the D166 again (**1h50min**), turn 90° right on a cart track between vineyards, making for a stone farm building ahead, behind a cypress tree. Two parallel cart tracks run towards this building; keep to the left-hand one. After passing to the left of the building, curl left on the track, rounding the vineyard. After a good 100m/yds (where the track curls half-left), take a *good, clear* path down right through trees (there are some minor, overgrown paths down right before this one.)

In two minutes you're on the shingle beach beside the **river Cèze** (**2h**), where you turn left upstream alongside the **Cascades du Sautadet**. (But if you plan to swim, do so now: it's forbidden at the falls.)

From here allow at least 30 minutes to walk back to your car. There's a good, shady path at the left of the falls (with pine-shaded picnic spots), but boulder-hopping is a must! At the top end of the falls, turn left to a lane and follow it back to the PARKING AREA below **La Roque** (**2h30min**).

Walk 10: GORGES DE L'ARDECHE

Distance: about 5km/3mi; 2h
Grade: fairly easy, but you must be sure-footed. *Only suitable after a period of settled dry weather; **dangerous** if wet.* If there has been heavy rain, the bedrock beside the gorge will take a couple of days to dry. Otherwise it can be difficult just to stand upright, and there are several awkward rock steps and ledges en route. Yellow and white waymarking, *which must be followed assiduously. IGN map 2939 OT*
Equipment: see page 68; refreshments at Sauze, Les Grottes
How to get there: 🚗 (optional detour on Car tours 4-7) to one of three starting points (see below). (Although 🚌 line 20 serves St-Martin, 2km from Sauze, there are no convenient buses at present; recheck at www.ardeche.fr/infrastructures-transports/transports-publics-voyageurs/horaires.)

We've dipped (almost literally) into this walk three times and found it surprisingly tiring. Perhaps we've been unlucky, with wet conditions and impassable fords. But *do* be prepared to make slower progress than you might expect of a riverside stroll! Much of the walk is over bedrock — as slippery as ice in wet conditions, and there are a few quite awkward rock ledges to scramble over.

Rather than give precise route descriptions and timings, we suggest three ways to start the walk, and how far you might reasonably hope to get. The map shows only a small section of the gorge; if you want to try to reach the Cirque de la Madelaine, the most dramatic meander in the gorge, buy the IGN map on site. All the starting points are off the main tourist road between Vallon Pont d'Arc and St-Just (D290) — easily reached as a detour during Car tours 4, 5 or 6.

1 Start out at the CAMP SITE at **Sauze** (paid parking). This is the most popular starting point, so will be *very* crowded on weekends and holidays. It is signposted off the D290 about 2km northwest of St-Martin d'Ardèche. A track leads to a sign, GORGES DE L'ARDECHE — RESERVE NATURELLE, where you turn down to the river. The most awkward points, if you begin here, are encountered below the **Ranc Pointu**

98

viewpoint, where the rock steps demand sure-footedness and caution, and at **Le Détroit**, where there is another awkward ledge to negotiate. From this starting point you might walk to the CAMP SITE **Les Grottes** and back (**2h30min**).

2 Start out 200m east of the **Ranc Pointu** viewpoint on the D290 (ample parking beside the road). From here a path descends 100m/330ft into a side-valley and then the main gorge (15min). Advantages: fewer people, free parking, avoids the steps at Ranc Pointu. Disadvantages: The final descent down a 4m/12ft-

Gorges de l'Ardèche near Sauze

Cirque de la Madelaine

high ledge is via iron rungs bolted into the rock, and you still encounter the awkward ledge at **Le Détroit**. When you reach the *CAMP SITE* of **Les Grottes** (**30min**) — and 'grotty' it is, with all the ghetto blasters and unclad bodies sprawled about — you're likely to find it closed off with tape. Just ignore the tapes and plough right through, averting your eyes. Continue as long as you like along the gorge — perhaps to the **Rapide de la Cadière** and back (**2h**).

3 Start out at the *BUVETTE* at **Les Grottes**. This is signposted off the D290 opposite the **Grotte de St-Marcel** and **Sentier botanique**, some 4km west of the Ranc Pointu viewpoint (1.5km down a dirt track). From here it's about 5km/3mi; 2h to the Cirque de la Madelaine, so you might make it! Then again, like us, you might find the ford 1.5km south of the *cirque* impassable! (Hint: the *Sentier botanique* at St-Marcel is enjoyable; allow 1h30min.)

Château de Barbentane (Walk 11)

Walk 11: BARBENTANE AND ST-MICHEL-DE-FRIGOLET

See also photograph opposite (bottom)
Distance: 10.5km/6.5mi; 3h (11.5km/7mi; 3h25min by bus)
Grade: easy, with ascents/descents of about 150m/5000ft overall. Some yellow PR way-marking, but route-finding can be tricky where waymarks are lacking. It helps to have a good sense of direction, as there are many woodland tracks. *IGN map 3042 OT*
Equipment: see page 68; refreshments available at the abbey (closed Mondays and January), or Barbentane
How to get there: 🚌 (Car tour 5; park in the centre or at the 8min-point and start the walk there) or 🚌 E1 from Nîmes or Avignon to Barbentane (www.stdgard.com/accueil/ horaires); alight/reboard at the 'St-Joseph' roundabout under 1km northeast of the centre.
Short walk: St-Michel-de-Frigolet (4.2km/2.6mi; 1h-10min). Easy. Access: 🚌 to the **Draille du Mas de la Dame**, a motorable track running south-east off the D35e, 2.2km north of the Abbey of Frigolet (Car tour 5). Large shaded parking area just at the start of this track. Follow the main walk from the 50min-point to the 2h-point, then keep straight ahead, back to your car.

The plain below La Montagnette, a pocket-sized mountain astride the Rhône, is the setting for a delightful walk through woodlands and beside flower-filled olive groves, with the option of a visit to the abbey of St-Michel-de-Frigolet and the charming village of Barbentane with its exquisite château.

Start out at the POSTE at **Barbentane**. Go through the ARCHWAY diagonally opposite: you look straight ahead to the 14th-century **Tour Angelica. Cross Rue du Four and Rue du Barry, then t**urn right to round the CHURCH. At the T-junction go right, then immediately left (⬆: VIEUX VILLAGE, MONTAGNETTE). Rise straight over a crossroads and go under another ARCHWAY. At a Y-fork, go right. The Tour Angelica is now just behind you, to your left. Keep straight ahead along **Chemin des Moulins,** passing an old wind-mill, the **Moulin de Brétoule** up left. At a T-junction, go right — to another T-junction facing a car park and WALKERS' SIGNBOARD (**8min**).

From the right-hand side of the car park, take the chained-off path just to the left of a house (yellow waymark and ⬆: MD200). Stay on this main path which rises and widens to a track. Ignore all turn-offs until you come to a major fork of tracks (**20min**), where you keep right uphill. Ingore a waymarked track off right four minutes later; keep ahead, passing a yellow 'X' on a tree on the left. Walk between a huge boulder (left) and a cottage (right). Three minutes later, as you pass under POWER LINES (**35min**), keep straight ahead, ignoring a track to the right and another running downhill to the left. Pass two tracks off left in quick succession, then take the *third*

St-Michel-de-Frigolet (top) and the Moulin de la Brétoule at Barbentane

turn left — *a dirt road which curves in front of you*. This comes down to the D35e at Mas de Roch. Turn right on the road and follow it to **Mas de Ferrier**. Just past here, turn left to a large shaded PARKING AREA at the start of a motorable track, the **Draille du Mas de la Dame** (**50min**).

From here head south on the stony track running not far to the left of the D35e; you pass *between* a WELL on the left and an SHRINE on the right almost at once. Just before this track rejoins the D35e, take a wide path on the left. Pass to the right of a large BUILDING FOUNDATION IN RUINS (**55min**), then turn left at a T-junction. After 30m/yds, go right uphill on another path in the **Bois de Barbentane** — the prettiest woodland path on the walk, almost jungle-like in places. After passing through a clearing and going round a wire barrier, cross the scruffy forestry works area, bearing right on a forestry track. From now on, *just keep to the left of the D35e,* whether on track or path. Go through a TALL HEDGE OF CYPRESSES and continue 250m/yds to the abbey of **St-Michel-de-Frigolet** (**1h20min**). Inside the lavishly decorated main church you'll find the original 11th-century abbey, now an apse off the north aisle. This little gem, the chapel of **Notre-Dame-du-Bon-Remède**, has beautiful gilt panelling. Then take some time to wander along the cobbled walkways, past the simple 12th-century church of **St-Michel** and around the grounds (with café).

After your visit, return to the CYPRESS HEDGE and turn right in front of it. At the end of the hedge, walk between posts, cross a path going left and then go half-left on a rising stony path. *Ignore* a clear path going sharply to the right. *Just 60 metres/yards from the cypresses,* turn sharp right down a clear but narrow path into a gully.* A pretty path through *maquis* takes you out of the gully, then dips again — to the hairpin bend of a track (**1h30min**). Turn right, beginning to round the **Mont de la Mère**. Ignore any paths to the left, unless you fancy the views from the top. Some 200m/yds from the hairpin bend there is an IMPORTANT JUNCTION: we used to go left here, but the landowner has fenced off access, so heed the yellow 'X' and *go right!* Head southeast for 300m/yds, then be sure to follow the track in a U-bend to the left, ignoring a track off right. You are now walking on the **Draille du Mas de la Dame**, first encountered at the 50min-point. You will see fencing on the left, then pass the landowner's property (a B&B) on the left and the **Mas de la Dame** on the right (**1h45min**). Some 900m further on (**2h**), *watch for the back of a road sign on your left* (it *may* bear a yellow 'X'): for the main walk, turn right here, then right again. *(But for the Short walk, keep straight ahead, back to your car.)*

---

*We prefer this pretty short-cut, but the 'official', yellow-waymarked route is highlighted in violet on the map.

Beyond an olive grove on the left you come to another *mas* and a junction: go left here, ignoring tracks to the right and straight ahead. Pass a second entrance to the same estate (on the left) and ignore a track to the right just opposite it. But at the next, Y-fork, go right. After 100m/yds, at a T-junction, go left. Pass a shed in a pretty grassy area on the right and come to crossroads at a clearing, with POWER LINES overhead. Keep straight ahead, downhill. When a track comes in from the left, behind you, keep right downhill. Walk to the left of a cherry orchard and under more POWER LINES. Just before an IRON CROSS (**Croix de Chaulet; 2h25min**), turn right on a country lane. Over to the left, across fields, you can see the Tour Angelica at Barbentane on a slight, wooded rise; dating from 1365, it's the keep of the former castle. Some 400m/yds along, turn left on a cart track (opposite a numbered FIRE TRACK). This route is a delight of colourful hedgerows and olive groves.

Just beyond **Mas de Bassette** (**2h45min**) go straight ahead on a tarred road, passing an IRON CROSS atop a mound on the right. Rise to a T-junction and turn left on the **Chemin Moulin de Brétoule** through a modern housing estate. Keep on this road past a FOOTBALL PITCH (behind cypresses on the left) and then an olive grove (also on the left). At another T-junction, with the OLD WINDMILL passed earlier up to the right (**2h50min**), either turn left to the CAR PARK or retrace your steps past the **Tour Angelica** to the POSTE in **Barbentane** (**3h**).

See also photographs on pages 34-35, 36
Distance: 15km/9.3mi; 4h15min for motorists; 21km/13mi; 6h for those travelling by bus to/from St-Rémy
Grade: moderate, with ascents/descents of 250m/820ft overall. The walk mostly follows tracks which are stony underfoot. *Not* recommended in hot weather, as there is almost no shade. Yellow PR and red and white GR waymarking, but some sections are *not waymarked. IGN map 3042 OT*
Equipment: see page 68. Refreshments available at Les Baux, halfway along
How to get there: 🚌 to the large parking area at the lake (Barrage des Peiroou) near St-Rémy. Follow the D5 south out of St-Rémy (Car tour 5). Note the km reading when you pass the tourist office (on your right); 0.5km further on, turn right for LAC DES PIEROOU, LE BARRAGE; the parking area is 2km further on. Or 🚌 57E to Les Baux (the 1h45min-point in the walk) and do the circuit from there. Also accessible by 🚌 57A and 🚌 54 to St-Rémy, but you will have to add an extra 6km/1h45min from there to the lake and back — or take a taxi to start and follow the end of Short walk 2 to return from the lake to St-Rémy. The best source of bus timetable information for both Les Baux and St-Rémy is the St-Rémy tourist office, www.saintremy-de-provence.com.
Short walks
1 St-Rémy — Les Baux. 6km/3.7mi; 2h. Grade as main walk, but the climb is under 150m/500ft. Follow the main walk to Les Baux and from

there catch a bus back to St-Rémy (add up to 3km/45min to walk on to your car at the lake) — or take a taxi back to the lake (the taxi rank is by the bus stop in Les Baux).
2 Les Baux — St-Rémy. 11km/6.8mi; 3h30min. Quite easy, with ascents of under 150m/500ft. Access by 🚌 (see above) or 🚗 to Les Baux. Follow the main walk from the 2h-point to the end at the Barrage des Pieroou. Facing the lake, take the wide gravel path signposted ST-REMY PAR LES ANTIQUES. *Be sure to keep right at a fork 50m/yds along:* (the GR6 route is very tricky). This rises and falls to the D5 just south of **Glanum**, where you turn left, passing **Les Antiques** (see page 35). Now, rather than keeping to the D5, take the road almost opposite Les Antiques, the **Chemin des Carrières** (with a fingerpost for EYGALIERES and a sign announcing that the 11th-century chapel and cloister of **St-Paul de Mausole** are open from 09.00 until 19.00). You now enter the 'Universe of Van Gogh', a walk devised by the St-Rémy Tourist Board and illustrated with 21 reproductions of Van Gogh's paintings. The artist was hospitalised at this convalescent home (it serves much the same function today and is considerably enlarged). From the chapel, walk back to Chemin des Carrières and turn left. By TABLEAU 8, turn left on a path, past a lovely property on the right. You join a lane, the grandly-named **Avenue Marie Gasquet**, and follow this past TABLEAUS 9-12. Go straight over a crossroads to TABLEAU 13 and now follow **Avenue**

Pierre Barbier to **Avenue Pasteur**. Turn right; the Tourist Office is just to your left, and all the good restaurants in St-Rémy are just a few steps away. The Tourist Office can advise on buses or call a taxi to take you back to your car at Les Baux.

Alternative route: Piste des Lombards. This PR-waymarked route is high-lighted in lilac on the map.

This delightful ridge walk is probably the most popular in the Alpilles, and deservedly so: it's not too long or too steep, and it leads from a gorgeous lake to one of the most famous beauty spots in France, the magnificently-sited citadel of Les Baux, shown on pages 34-35. Les Antiques and Glanum are close to the lake where the walk begins and ends, so plan to spend the whole day in this area.

Start out at the lake, the **Barrage des Peiroou**, much favoured by picnickers and anglers. Notice, off to the right, as you face the lake, a wide gravel path signposted 'St-Rémy par les Antiques': if you came by bus from St-Rémy, you will return that way. Retrace your steps from the lake for a couple of minutes, until the GR6 turns left on a level earthern forestry track (currently marked AL113). Ignore this; keep on the road for another 150m/yds, then turn left uphill on a stony track (currently marked AL112).

The Barrage des Peiroou, where the walk begins

After about 12 minutes, a PR path waymarked in yellow goes off to the left: ignore this path too; follow the track round to the right, to a tarred area with a CISTERN (**15min**). Continue straight ahead along the tar, ignoring a track descending to the right. Looking left now, you'll see the huge ORTF relay equipment on the bluff of La Caume.

Ignore paths to the right and then left; keep on the main track, which bends sharply to the right. You enjoy good views to the north, before the track turns southwards again. At this point (**30min**) the main track continues ahead, but we fork right uphill on a footpath — which may have both red and white GR waymarks and yellow PR waymarks. (This path gives super views of the north from a crest. If you prefer to avoid the climb, or if a *mistral* is blowing, stay on the track and fork right when you quickly come to a T-junction.) So far the ascent has been imperceptible, but now we *do* climb. In about six minutes we reach the top with its fine views and gale-force winds. Five minutes later we're back down on the main track. Continue southwest along the main track now, ignoring a minor cart track going off to the right. Two minutes along ignore a numbered fire track coming in from the left and then a track off right to the fire watchtower (**Tour de Guet**); continue straight ahead.

Now we are going to part company with the GR and take a much more attractive path. This path is *not waymarked*, so follow the notes carefully. Five minutes past the track up to the watchtower (**55min**) the main track describes a deep U-bend, and you come to a junction of paths and tracks: a path comes down from the watchtower on the right, and another path goes out left to a triangulation point. Leave the main track here (it is the return route): take the track to the left of the main track, but to the right of the path to the triangulation point. You are

walking parallel with the main track, but descending. After about 100m/yds downhill, turn left on another track — the first one you come to. Now you're heading in the direction of the triangulation point, and soon the track becomes a lovely grassy footpath. Not far along, a path comes down from the triangulation point and joins you from the left.

After descending for about 15 minutes, meet a wide stony crossing path (**1h15min**) and turn left; you may see some fluorescent orange waymarks underfoot. In two minutes go round a chain barrier, then meet another track and turn left (above a house where there may be an *unchained* dog). Pass two houses on the right and immediately come to a tarred junction. Turn right, gradually descending. An alternative route, waymarked in yellow, comes in from the left after 600m/yds (see lilac lines on the map), and 100m/yds further on you meet the D27a (**1h30min**). Now you have to follow this road just over 1.5km uphill to **Les Baux**, but all along the road there are fine views to the bauxite mines and Les Baux rising on the cliffs.

Continue uphill to the parking area below Les Baux and walk past the PARKING ATTENDANT'S STONE KIOSK (**2h**; BUS STOP, TAXI RANK). Up on your left, before you come to the main village gate, is a shop selling snacks and drinks — a great pit stop on a hot day, especially if you don't want to join the midday crowds at the citadel. The tourist Office is just inside the gate, on the left; next door is a super restaurant.

From the shop (or gate) walk back downhill past the parking attendant's kiosk and, when you are back on the D27a, turn left downhill towards FONT-VIEILLE and ARLES. Joining the D27, go right, ignoring the left turn for Fontvieille and Arles. Soon you pass the **Cathédral des Images** and some bauxite mines. Just beyond the sign denoting the EXIT FROM LES BAUX (**2h20min**), turn right on a track and walk to the right of a chain barrier (prohibiting vehicles). After climbing for less than 15 minutes, come to a T-junction with a stony track and turn left, still climbing (here you join a PR route way-marked in yellow). Three minutes uphill you round a bend and have a most magnificent view over to the left, across the Val d'Enfer and to Les Baux: the old mines are in foreground on other side of valley, with the village and the citadel behind them. The gentle Vallon de la Font

Outlook from the vandalised viewing table at the 2h45min-point across the Val d'Enfer to Les Baux

point (**3h15min**) you rejoin your outgoing route, when you round the U-bend below the fire watchtower. Five minutes later pass the track up to the watchtower and two minutes after that the path you descended from the ridge-top viewpoint; keep right along the track here. Three minutes later, where a fainter track goes downhill to the right, keep left with the red and white flashes of the GR6 along the level track. It curls around to offer a superb view of the Alpilles and La Caume. Three minutes another path climbs up left to the ridge-top viewpoint; keep to the track, which curves to the right. You come to a ROCK CUTTING; if you turn down left here, you can descend along your outgoing route, saving about 15-20 minutes).

The main walk continues past the cutting, still following the GR6. Looking down left through the trees, soon you will spot the lake where you set out, with the spire of St-Rémy's church behind it. Ignore any grassy tracks downhill either side of the main track. The downhill track you want comes up about 20 minutes past the cutting (**3h55min**) — only about 150m/yds short of the D5. Head downhill with the red and white flashes of the GR6, as the track which you have been following continues ahead to the D5. This pine-shaded, stony track takes you to the tarmac road to the lake, where you turn right downhill to the **Barrage des Peiroou** (**4h15min**).

spreads out to the right of the citadel.

Some 25 minutes off the D27 cross straight over a tarmac road and climb the steep path opposite to a fine viewpoint (**2h45min**). There was a beautiful *table d'orientation* here for many years, but it's been vandalised — chiselled clean off its base (no doubt someone wanted a unique and classy coffee table). Unless it is very hazy, you will have good views of the Camargue and the Rhône Valley, the Lubéron and Mont Ventoux.

From the viewpoint walk down the wide track. Join the tarmac road and follow it to the left. When the road runs out, keep straight ahead on a tarmac lane, behind a chain barrier. Stalwart yellow mullein blooms here in summer. Five minutes along, at a Y-fork, ignore the concreted fire point up to the right; keep left along the track. Ten minutes later ignore the overgrown track on the right; keep left on the main track.

Half an hour from the view-

Walk 13: LE DESTET AND AUREILLE

See photograph page 111
Distance: 7.5km/4.7mi;
2h30min
Grade: easy, with ascent/
descent of about 100m/330ft
overall, but there is *no shade*.
Some yellow PR waymarking,
some red and white GR waymarking. *IGN map 3043 OT*
Equipment: see page 68;
refreshments available at
Aureille
How to get there: 🚌 to Le
Destet (southeast of St-Rémy,
Car tour 5). From the junction
of the D78 and D24 drive
south towards Mouriès along
the D24 and after 200m turn
left on the first track you come
to (one of the signs here adver-
tises organic olive oil for sale at
the Moulin de Vaudoret).
Continue uphill for about
0.8km and park off the side of
the track when you are level
with the far end of the moto-
cross circuit. Or 🚐 029 from
Arles to Salon via Aureille;

pick up the main walk at the
1h05min-point; follow it to
the end and then walk back to
Aureille using the notes at the
start of the walk (timetables
can be downloaded at www.
lepilote.com.
Short walk: Vaudoret.
4.5km/ 2.8mi; 1h35min. Easy,
with minimal ascents. Follow
the main walk for 40min, then
turn right downhill. Pick up
the notes again after the
1h35min-point.
**Alternative walk: Le Destet
— Tour des Opies — Le
Destet.** 15km/9.4mi;
5h20min. Strenuous and long,
with an overall ascent/descent
of 450m/1475ft. Follow this
walk to Aureille (1h05min).
After stopping for refreshments, pick up Walk 14. On
your return to Aureille from
the Tour des Opies, take
another break, then continue
this walk from the 1h05min-
point.

Silvery leaves glisten beneath a porcelain-blue sky,
and the air shimmers with heat, as you walk to the
pretty village of Aureille and then through olive groves
typical of the Alpilles. Choose a cool day between October and May for this countryside ramble *in full sun*. For
the really fit, the Alternative walk is a magnificent hike,
and all the more manageable because you can take a
break in Aureille on both the outward and return legs.

Start out by trudging east
along the track from the *MOTO-
CROSS CIRCUIT* where you
parked. Ignore the tracks off
right to the farm of Vaudoret
(**5min, 15min**). We'll delve
into the Vaudoret olive groves
later in the walk. At the next,
three-way junction (under
20min) take the middle track
or the one on the left (they
rejoin); the track on the right is
our return route. Four minutes
later, ignore a track left uphill

but, three minutes further on,
at a Y-fork, *do* go left (and
ignore a path off to the right a
minute uphill). This track
skirts to the right of a
cultivated field, then brushes
up against the cliffs we have
been following since starting
out. Notice the turpentine
trees (*Pistacia terebinthus*), with
their shiny leaves and autumn
clusters of reddish-brown
fruits.
You eventually approach a

couple of BUILDINGS on the left (**35min**). Continue past them on a very overgrown track. It loops away from the cliff wall and skirts a field full of thistles. Keep to the left-hand side of the field; a stream is on your left. On meeting a stronger crossing track, under four minutes past the buildings, turn left, crossing the STREAM. A minute later (**40min**), ignore a strong track coming in from the left; keep straight ahead. But notice, almost immediately, the good track down right into the olive groves — your return route. *(The Short walk goes right here.)* Now ignore a track off to the right; continue ahead over a rushing WATERCOURSE. Keep ahead past another track off right, soon coming to a crest with a fine view ahead to Aureille, crowned by its château. A beautiful rounded mountain with a tower rises behind the village: Les Opies — the highest point in the Alpilles (Alternative walk). Tar comes underfoot at a housing estate, where you join the GR6. When you come to a Y-fork, bear right on **Rue du Batiment**. Turn right to cross the pretty stream, and then go left towards the CLOCK TOWER in the centre of **Aureille**; a bar/café is just opposite. Walk past the clock tower and turn right into the lovely CHURCH SQUARE (**1h05min**).

Leaving the square, go back to the main road (**Avenue Mistral**). Facing the 'PRESSE'

SHOP, head left. Walk the short distance to the **Place de la Fontaine**, then turn right on the D25a (signposted to Les Baux and St-Rémy). Then, almost immediately, turn left to cross the stream. You now leave Aureille the way you came in (Rue du Batiment), with the red and white GR flashes. Follow this to a Y-fork and keep right with the GR6 on the **Chemin de St-Jean**. When the tar ends and the GR turns up right, note the time. In under 10 minutes you will cross the RUSHING WATER-COURSE again. Just beyond it, ignore a first track off left, but turn left on the next track, into the **Vaudoret** olive groves (**1h35min**).

Down in the heart of the groves, you meet a T-junction after 15 minutes: turn right into a quintessential Alpilles setting, with olive groves in the foreground and a backdrop of limestone cliffs. As the track curls round to the right, back towards the cliffs, the way is brighted by bright pinky-purple cranesbill (*Geranium tuberosum*) and Scottish thistles.

When you rejoin your outgoing route at the three-way fork (**2h20min**), turn left. Now that you are nearer your car, you may want to stop in at the Vaudoret Mill to buy some of their prize-winning olive oil, if it's open. Otherwise it's only 10 minutes back to your car near the MOTO-CROSS CIRCUIT (**2h30min**).

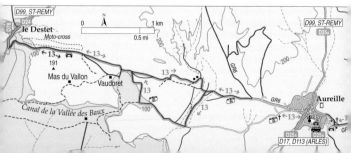

Walk 14: TOUR DES OPIES

Distance: 8.5km/5.3mi; 3h05min

Grade: moderate ascent of 350m/1150ft, but you must be sure-footed and agile. Do not attempt the summit on windy days. Although the path is well used, be prepared to push through prickly broom. Little shade. GR waymarking at the start; variable waymarking to the pass; *no* waymarking to the summit. *IGN map 3043 OT*

Equipment: see page 68; suitable clothing for dense undergrowth; walking stick(s). Refreshments available at Aureille

How to get there: 🚌 (as Walk 13; see page 109) or 🚗 to Aureille (on the D25a, 12km from Le Destet; detour on Car tour 5). Park in or near the church square (or park at the cemetery below the village, saving 1km/15min walking time by picking up the walk at

Church at Aureille (Walks 13 and 14)

the 7min-point, following the GR signs for 'Eyguieres, Lamanon').

O ne of our favourite hikes, this gorgeous, varied walk leads through dense *maquis,* with a huge variety of wild flowers, and a fairy-tale wood, before struggling up to a restored Saracen tower with panoramic views.

Start out facing the 'PRESSE' SHOP on the main street in **Aureille** (**Avenue Mistral**), just north of the CHURCH SQUARE. Walk left, past the CLOCK TOWER on the right, to the **Place de la Fontaine**, then turn right on the D25a (signposted to Les Baux and St-Rémy), crossing the stream. Very quickly you come to an old WASH-HOUSE, with

Aureille's ruined castle rising above it. This is **Place du Lavoir**. Three narrow roads lead out of this square: take the middle one, the **Rue du Lavoir**. Follow this uphill, just at the right of and below the CASTLE. At **Place du Château** fork left, uphill — you can see Aureille's church over to your right. You're now on **Rue de la Savoie**; this becomes a cart track and runs above and to the left of the CEMETERY. At the far side of the cemetery, ignore a first gravel track off left (by a SHRINE on the left), but at the next track, almost immediately,

111

turn left. There are two GR SIGNPOSTS here (**7min**); follow the one for EYGUIERES, LAMANON, ignoring the route to the right towards Eygalières and Mouriès. Your track heads due east (past a barrier blocking motor traffic) towards the tower atop the Opies.

At a Y-fork after some 250m, bear left, *leaving* the GR (**15min**; there may be a painted ARROW here). Follow this track, skirting just to the left of an ANIMAL ENCLOSURE WITH TREES, being sure to ignore a track off to the left. The stony track swings round to the right and narrows (**35min**). (At this point,

ignore a path to the left.)

Be prepared now to push your way through tall thickets of pricky broom; the path itself is very clear underfoot. At a Y-fork (**55min**) keep right (WAYMARK on a stone) and rise through the welcome shade of a dense woodland bower.

On reaching the PASS below the tower (**1h15min**; HUGE CAIRN), you enjoy a superb view north to the Vallon de Valdelègue; the tower is up to your right. From here take the path running sharply up to the right; it soon frays out into many strands (avoid minor short-cut paths to the left), but your goal is obvious. The path rounds the southwest side of the summit, comes to another huge CAIRN, then heads hard left. Just *before* reaching the METAL POLE below the tower, turn up *right* for the easiest final scramble.

From the **Tour des Opies** (**1h40min**) the views are tremendous, taking in Aureille far below, the Alpilles, La Caume with its transmitter, the Etang de Berre and Mediterranean in the south, and — conditions permitting — Ste-Victoire to the east and even Mont Ventoux to the north!

Retrace your steps from here to the CEMETERY and follow the Rue de la Savoie uphill. Just past where the road becomes tarred, turn down left to the main road. Then go right to the 'PRESSE' SHOP in the centre of **Aureille** (**3h05min**). The alley opposite the shop leads to the CHURCH SQUARE.

The flower-filled summit ascent path (top), and a view to Aureille and La Caume, not far below the top

Walk 15: DIGUE A LA MER

See also photographs page 40
Distance: 7.5km/4.7mi; 2h15min
Grade: easy, level walk along stony tracks. But flat walks along blinding-white tracks where there is no shade can be surprisingly tiring. We would not recommend any walks longer than 2-3 hours in the Camargue. Rent a bicycle instead! *No* waymarking. *IGN map 2944 OT.*
Equipment: see page 68; trainers will suffice. *Adequate sun protection is mandatory; the cool breeze is deceptive, and sunstroke is a real possibility.* If you take a picnic, remember that any food here will probably attract swarms of insects. The nearest village for refreshments is Salin-de-Giraud, but first try the B&Bs at Le Paradis or nearby St-Bertrand.
How to get there: 🚗 to the pumping station between the Etang du Fangassier and the Etang de Galabert (accessible from Villeneuve on the D37 — the 146km-point in Car tour 6; see notes on pages 40-41). Outside winter, the car will be a furnace on your return. No 🚌 service.

The circuit on the north side of the Etang de Galabert is a good introduction to the Camargue, one of the very few places in the Mediterranean where flamingoes breed. Not only will you see your fill of flamingoes (45,000 individuals have been recorded here), but a great many other birds as well.

Start out at the PUMPING STATION between the **Galabert and Fangassier lagoons**. (The flamingoes breed on an islet in the Fangassier Lagoon, and from April to July their raised conical nests are under round-the-clock surveillance by the park and reserve authorities.) Follow the dyke (**Digue à la Mer**) northwest; the pump will be just on your left as you set off — churning away, with any luck. The lighthouse

View back to the Phare de la Gachole from the sand-bar

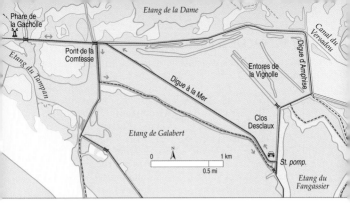

(Phare de la Gacholle) glimmers in the distance.

Spiny glassworts (*Salicornia* species) predominate, peppered by the odd wizened-up daisies, thistles and purple-flowering knautia. The track is embedded with tiny, perfectly-formed sea shells. A fairly stagnant strip of water is on your left and a narrow sand-bar beyond it; this will be the return route. The muted pinks and purples in the still water and the dull greens and yellows of the surface algae create beautiful abstract patterns. By the side of the path an inter-mittent double row of wooden posts helps to shore up the dyke; a sludge of salty foam clings to them. The monotony is broken only by the screeching of myriad seagulls swirling above an islet to the left.

Eventually you reach the **Pont de la Comtesse** (**45min**), an important level-changing station. Cars are not allowed beyond this point, and walkers/cyclists are reminded to keep to the track. Passing the **Etang du Tampan** on the left, you come to the **Phare de la Gacholle** (**1h**), graced by a purple-flowering tamarisk, a fine specimen of the most characteristic tree in the Camargue. The surrounds of this inhabited lighthouse are closed.

Return to the Pont de la Comtesse and turn right on a wide track. Some 500m/yds along, be sure to turn left onto the sand-bar, not far beyond a barrier. (If you continue ahead, you would have to round the entire Etang de Galabert, a *very* long walk indeed.) This path, lined with gold grasses and sprouting huge yellow oyster plants with thistle-like leaves, runs down the middle of the sand-bar. While you wait for a flamingo to spread its black and salmon-red wings within camera range, be sure to watch your feet or you're likely to trip up on one of the hundreds of huge rabbit holes. Opposite 'shriek island', still swirling with gulls, you come across the colony of sneezeworts (*Achillea*) shown on page 113. When you approach the PUMPING STATION, turn right to cross a BRIDGE; then, about 20m/yds beyond it, turn left on a track, back to your car (**2h15min**).

Walk 16: MONTCALMES, AND A VIEW OVER ST-GUILHEM-LE-DESERT

Distance: 13.5km/8.4mi; 3h45min

Grade: easy-moderate, with ascents/descents of 175m/575ft overall. Stony tracks throughout, and virtually *no shade* en route. Variable waymarking, including some yellow PR flashes. *IGN maps 2642 ET*

Equipment: see page 68; refreshments available at Puéchabon

How to get there: 🚌 to the Bergerie Neuve. Leave the D32 at the calvary on the south side of Puéchabon (Car tour 7): take the road at the right of the calvary (as you face it), then turn right immediately on a lane (Route de Lavène). Follow it for 2.3km, until it ends at a building (the Bergerie Neuve). No 🚌 service nearby at time of writing; you can check at www.herault-transport.fr, where there is a downloadable map of bus routes.

Short walk: Bergerie Neuve — Montcalmès — Bergerie Neuve. 5km/3mi; 1h05min. Easy climb and descent of 85m/280ft. Follow the main walk for 35min and return the same way.

This walk across a limestone plateau *(causse)* above the Gorges de l'Hérault takes us through *garrigues* bristling with holm and kermes oaks to the magnificent viewpoint over St-Guilhem-le-Désert shown on page 117. With each footstep we move back in time … to the 8th century, when Charlemagne was on the throne.

Start out at the **Bergerie Neuve**: take the motorable track furthest to the left and climb to the hamlet of **Lavène** (**15min**). Today there are only a couple of inhabited buildings spilling out window-boxes fresh with colour, but in the 8th century Lavène was a *cité*.

Continue on the main track, heading straight towards St-Baudille (with the large relay station), one of the peaks of the Séranne massif. Ten minutes along you pass a *lavogne* on the left-hand side of the track (a paved watering hole for animals; **Lac Neuf** on

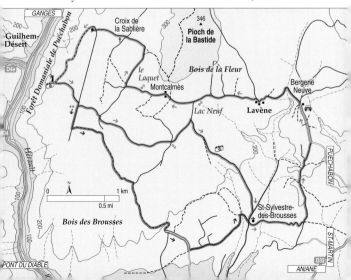

the map). Just beyond it, at a Y-fork, keep right. This very stony track takes you to the ruined fortified hamlet of **Montcalmès** (**35min**). The huge château here also dates from the 8th century and was given by Charlemagne to St Benoit. The very substantial remains include arches, doorways, a well-preserved *bergerie* and a baking oven. There is shade and grass; it makes a superb picnic spot, where you can end the Short walk. Be sure to explore the ruins *carefully;* some of the masonry is unstable.

Continuing on the track, five minutes beyond Montcalmès you pass a second, semi-circular *lavogne* on the right (**Le Laquet**). Now St-Baudille and the mountains behind St-Guilhem seem very close indeed. Three minutes past the *lavogne* ignore a track off to the left. Half a minute later, ignore a second track off left; keep to the obvious main track, ignoring offshoots. You eventually pass an IRON CROSS on the left, some 30m/yds away (**Croix de la Sablière; 55min**). The track runs alongside masses of small rock quarries before reaching the WESTERN EDGE OF THE PLATEAU (just over **1h05min**), from where the view towards the Séranne improves.

There is a three-way fork here. Ignore the track straight ahead *and* the main track (marked with a huge cairn) which swings left and heads south-west in a straight line. Locate instead the small marker-stone to the right and take the narrow footpath to the right of it. This path quickly swings left and skirts the edge of the plateau. From time to time a cart track impinges on the path, but you can see the TV relay where you are heading. Keep an eye out for the turpentine and mastic trees (*Pistacia terebinthus* and *Pistacia lentiscus*), growing amidst the holm and holly oaks. Their red-to-black berries feed the birds that winter here. Foliage has grown up around the RELAY STATION (**1h30min**), so potter about until you can find an open viewpoint from which to savour the exquisite view shown opposite. St-Guilhem lies far below, a river of salmon-coloured rooftops flowing through the Combe de Gellone, below the menacing cliffs of the Cirque de l'Infernet. The rounded apse of the abbey church (all that remains of the original monastery founded by St-Guilhem) is clearly visible. (The church still displays its most precious relic — a piece of the true cross, given by Charlemagne to his friend Guilhem when the monastery was founded in 804.)

Take the track leading away from the relay. In three minutes ignore a track off to the left; it rejoins your track a minute later (just past a small but deep PIT on the left). After another two minutes, join the main track and go right, coming to a GREEN WATER TANK with the sign '**Forêt Domaniale de Puéchabon**' on your right in one minute. Turn left here. (*The track straight ahead is an alternative, equally attractive route, indicated by a lilac line on the map.*)

Five minutes later, at a T-junction, turn right. A minute later ignore a track off right. You come to a crossing track, where there is another

GREEN WATER TANK on the right (under **2h05min**); keep straight ahead here. Ignore a track on the right a minute later (it rejoins the main track). But six minutes past the water tank (**2h10min**), when you are almost back to the first *lavogne* on your outgoing route, turn right on a very stony track marked with a CAIRN (and a YELLOW FLASH about 20m/yds along).

This track rises slightly before descending steeply. There are fine views south to Aniane and the Hérault once you have cleared the trees and are approaching a vast spread of vineyards. Like the abbey church at St-Guilhem, **St-Sylvestre-des-Brousses**

(**2h50min**) was an important stop along the pilgrims' route to Santiago de Compostela. Head left downhill on the track behind the chapel. *(Or, if you came by the alternative route, keep straight ahead downhill.)* You climb to a crossing track, from where Puéchabon is visible to the right (**3h10min**). Turn left and keep climbing gently, now following RED WAYMARKS (and GREEN POSTS). When you come to a fork, where the waymarking posts and a cairn direct you to the right, keep *left*. At the next fork, a minute later, go right. Rejoining the little lane to the *bergerie*, turn left back to the **Bergerie Neuve (3h45min)**.

St-Guilhem, seen from the plateau

Walk 17: ON THE SHOULDERS OF PIC ST-LOUP

Distance: 4.5km/2.8mi; 2h
Grade: easy, gradual ascent/descent of 200m/650ft on a very stony track. Exploring the ruins demands agility and a head for heights (supervise small children carefully). Little shade. Some GR waymarking; other sections *not* waymarked. *IGN map 2742 ET*
Equipment: see page 68; refreshments available at St-Mathieu
How to get there: 🚗 to St-Mathieu-de-Tréviers (a detour from Car tour 7). Where Car tour 7 turns back at the fork to Valflaunès, keep ahead and, at the roundabout, turn right on the D17. After 1.5km, take the first exist from another roundabout. Now *carefully* follow CHATEAU DE MONTFERRAND and SENTIER DU PIC DE ST LOUP through a convoluted one-way system. After

a deep hairpin bend to the right, at the entrance to the upper village, keep left. Then go left again (in front of a large iron gate). Now you are on a narrow road which climbs to the Château St-Aunès. At the entrance (🚶: PIC ST-LOUP, CHATEAU DE MONTFERRAND, ACCES PEDESTRE), turn right on the track (large parking area 100m downhill). No 🚌 service at time of writing; you can check at www.herault-transport.fr.

Alternative walk: Pic St-Loup summit. 6.5km/4mi; 3h30min. Strenuous ascent/descent of 500m/ 1650ft; you must be sure-footed. Follow the main walk to the 35min-point, then keep left on the GR. The final ascent begins from the cross at **La Croisette** and follows an old pilgrims' trail to the chapel at the top.

There are several walks around Pic St-Loup, of which the PR route shown on IGN maps rounding the mountain and taking in the summit is probably the finest. But it takes a good five-six hours, and there is very little shade in this area. We prefer to look at the peak from a distance, from where its fine spinnaker-shaped wedge of rock can best be appreciated. This walk, to the Château de Montferrand, shows you the best of Pic St-Loup and its twin, Hortus, as well as affording far-reaching views to the Pyrenees and Mont Ventoux!

The Terrieu Valley, with St-Loup at the left and Hortus to the right

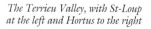

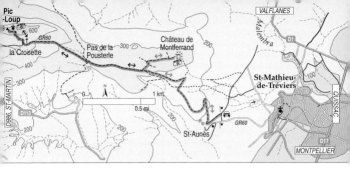

Start out at the PARKING AREA, following the red and white flashes of the GR60 (❘) along a stony track. You're into the climb straight away. Just before a concrete RESERVOIR (**5min**), turn right up a stony trail through the *garrigues,* where white Montepllier *Cistus* is particularly prominent. Keep to the very stony GR, ignoring any smaller paths off right or left. From time to time you will see the imposing château ahead or catch glimpses of the cross atop Pic St-Loup. When you come to a small CLEARING (**35min**), the GR continues ahead as an earthen path (*Alternative walk*). Turn right uphill here (*no way-*

marking) on another very stony trail. In three minutes you come to a fork, where you must turn *sharp left uphill —* even though you can see the château straight ahead. Two minutes later make another hairpin turn to the right, where a very narrow path goes straight ahead.

You come to a fork with a LARGE ROCK in the centre (**50min**), on which a plea to not discard litter is painted in blue. You *can* fork left here and climb over the rubble for a preliminary view over the plain and to Hortus, but the best way up to the ruins lies to the *right* of the stone. This route leads to a section of ruined wall

Pic St-Loup from the Château de Montferrand

where you can get a foothold. From there a fairly strong path leads *almost* all the way to the top. Clamber around the ruins of the **Château de Montferrand** (**1h**) carefully, admiring the vaulted rooftops remaining, the water deposits, the various keep walls.

From here you look north down into the lovely Terrieu Valley, where the cliffs of the Montagne d'Hortus rise behind Mas Rigaud. In the far distance the Cévennes shimmer in a blue haze. On a clear day, Mont Ventoux is visible in the east while, to the west, beyond the shoulder of St-Loup, you can see the huge relay station on St-Baudille in the Séranne massif (photograph page 117), and the Pyrenees in the far distance. In the south you

120

overlook the plains of Montpellier all the way to the coast and the buildings of La Grande Motte. Swallows swoop all round you.

This château was one of seven which Raymond VI of Toulouse was forced to surrender during the crusade against the Albigensians (see panel on page 62).

When you decide to leave, be sure you redescend via the wall with the foothold. (If you find yourself on what appears to be a good but stony path descending due south, you have gone wrong. This path *does* rejoin the GR, but it is very difficult.) Retrace your steps to the PARKING AREA (**2h**).

Walk 18: SOURCE OF THE VIS

See also photographs pages

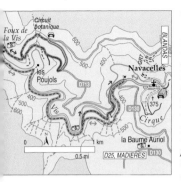

8-9 and 48-49
Distance: 8km/5mi; 2h40min
Grade: fairly easy, with

ascents/descents of about 100m/330ft overall. A few stretches demand agility. Some red/white GR, some red/yellow GRP, some yellow PR waymarking. *IGN map 2642 ET*
Equipment: see page 68; swimming things; refreshments available in Navacelles
How to get there: 🚌 to the Auberge de la Cascade in Navacelles (Car tour 8). *Or park at the 10min-point (see text).* No 🚐 service
Short walk: Banks of the Vis. 4km/2.5mi; 1h10min. Grade as main walk. Follow the main walk for about 35min and

This walk is perfect for a hot day; there's some shade en route, and the surging source of the river Vis at the end of the walk is blissfully cooling. This crystal-clear river is also an ideal swimming-hole, so take a picnic and plan to spend much of the day by its banks.

Start out at the Auberge de la Cascade in **Navacelles**. Cross the road to the POST BOX. Take the lane at the left of the post box (GR7 ☞: BLANDAS 4,5KM, RED/WHITE WAYMARKING). The lane skirts to the left of the river. Take the first left turn off the lane (sign: GITE D'ETAPE). Pass the CHURCH on the right and continue uphill on a narrow lane, walking to the right of a rounded wall with a waymark. When you come to the road, turn right. This slog up tarmac is unpleasant in hot weather, but you quickly come to the top of the climb, at a junction (**10min**). Here the D130 goes left to St-Maurice and the D713 ahead to Blandas. In between them is a footpath (☞: LES MOULINS DE LA FOUX), indicating that the source of the Vis is 1h away (for the *very* fleet of foot!). You could park here if there's room,

Grassy verge beside the river some 35 minutes into the walk.

saving 20 minutes on both the short and main walks — as well as the initial climb.
Follow the path between the roads; it's marked with both YELLOW PR and RED/ YELLOW GRP waymarks (it's part of the

121

GRP 'Tour du Larzac'). The path leads gently downhill past bright yellow broom, which flowers from April to July. After passing above a DAM (**20min**) the undulating path narrows. Sometimes you are quite high above the river so, although the drop is not sheer, watch your footing. Various bell-flowers are among the flora brightening this shady bower. Ten minutes later you descend very steeply to a T-junction with another path, where you turn left.

This is a lovely earthen path, pleasantly free of stones for the moment. The river is singing over on your right and, a minute along, you join it at a *GRASSY VERGE* (**35min**), a fine picnic spot. But before you settle for the day, continue just a short way further — to

another gorgeous spot, where flat slabs of rock jut out into the river (unless the river is running very high). This is an ideal spot to launch yourself for a swim and sunbathe afterwards. Damsel- and dragonflies in fluorescent hues dart about here, vying with the cornflower blue, orange, and yellow butterflies for attention; but most spectacular are the moths, their wings an intricate pattern of scarlet, teal blue and black. Until you reach the source, this is the most beautiful part of the walk.

Soon the path is somewhat overgrown and climbs away from the river. Eventually you pass the abandoned farmhouse of **Les Poujols** on the right (**1h05min**). On cool days, this open area makes a pleasant sun-trap for a picnic. A

The Vis surges through an 18th-century mill at its source (restored since this photograph was taken). Incredibly, this torrent suddenly ceased in April 1776. One can imagine the fear of the local people — who not only depended upon the Vis, but upon the mighty Hérault, which it feeds. Eight days later, as inexplicably as it had ceased, the source boiled over its cauldron again.

magnificent cedar forest comes into view on the opposite riverbank ten minutes later. (A *Circuit botanique* signposted from the D713 descends to the source through this forest; see Car tour 8 and lilac lines on the map.)

Ten minutes past Les Poujols, turn right downhill (▐: *LA FOUX*; **1h15min**). It's a steep descent of a few minutes to an OLD MILL, from where you'll have to scramble for another minute to enjoy the view of the source shown above. The atmosphere in this roaring green cauldron is wonderfully invigorating.

As you climb back up from the source, the enormous cliffs of the Causse du Larzac tower above you. In 45 minutes you will be back at the place where rocks jut out into the river. Just past the grassy verge, *be sure to climb uphill to the right on your outgoing path;* there *are* waymarks here, but they are easily missed. (The path straight ahead, indicated on the map by a lilac line, leads to a ford over to the dam passed earlier and then a track out onto the road, but the river can only be forded in summer.)

In 1h10min from the mill you should be back at the road junction. If you are staying overnight in Navacelles (apart from the Auberge de la Cascade, there is also a *gîte d'étape*), and you do this walk late in day, you'll come back into the village hugging yourself with the knowledge that you have this whole magnificent amphitheatre *almost* all to yourself. High up to the right, on the plateau, you can spot the restaurant of La Baume Auriol, from where you probably first saw the *cirque*. When the road curves round, and the statue on the hillock in the 'moat' is just ahead of you, turn down the tarred lane that you climbed at the start of the walk. Retrace your steps to the *auberge* in **Navacelles** (**2h40min**).

Walk 19: MONTPELLIER-LE-VIEUX

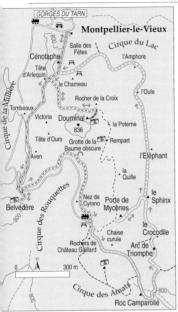

Distance: 5.5km/3.4mi; 2h15min

Grade: moderate ups and downs of about 150m/490ft, requiring agility. Good shade. Multi-coloured waymarking. *IGN map 2641 OT*

Equipment: see page 68; nearest refreshments at Millau; seasonal kiosk at the site

How to get there: 🚌 to Montpellier-le-Vieux (a detour on Car tour 8; see panel on page 50). Paid parking includes a plan *(note: north is at the bottom!)*. No 🚐 at time of writing; re-check at www.tourisme-aveyron.com or www.keolis-aveyron.com. *Note:* At www.montpellierle vieux.com (English pages) there are some good photographs of the rock formations and a video of the site.

Montpellier-le-Vieux is a *ruiniform* chaos writ large — the largest in Europe and since 2011 a UNESCO World Heritage Site. Our suggested walk takes in four of the five different routes (waymarked with coloured cubes on the ground). Pack a picnic and plan to spend at least half a day enjoying not only the rock formations, but the splendid woodlands and luxuriant displays of mosses, ferns … and wild flowers in spring.

Start out at the PARKING AREA: go up the path (⌐: CIRCUITS). Ignore the orange path forking left (our return route), but take the next left, the RED PATH to the **Douminal (15min)**, a rock tower overlooking the four *cirques* of the chaos. In the north is the thickly-forested Cirque du Lac, with the cliffs of the Gorges du Tarn rising in the distance.

From here *retrace your steps* to the RED/BLUE PATH and follow it to the left, to the **Belvédère (40min)** overlooking the **Cirque de la Millière**. Walk back over the bridge and turn right on the RED PATH, following it *across* the turning circle for the little train and a pleasant picnic area on the right.

Ignore the purple path off to the right here but, a minute later, fork right on the YELLOW PATH. The **Roc Camparolié** is the most dramatic formation on this stretch. You pass a narrow path off to the right (not signposted; it leads to the village of La-Roque-Ste-Marguerite in 1h), then descend to a clearing, where the **Arc de Triomphe** is ahead. Just past here, at a T-junction, go right (passing the **Crocodile** up on the right. From the **Sphinx** (**1h25min**), curl hard left to the **Porte de Mycènes**, shown below. Return to the Sphinx but, just before it, take the narrow ORANGE PATH, past the **Eléphant**. When you come to a Y-fork, keep left through the picnic area overlooking the **Cirque du Lac**, then fork right on the BLUE/RED PATH, back to the CAR PARK (**2h15min**).

Porte de Mycènes; below left: the Sphinx

Walk 20: SENTIER DE LA VALLÉE DU TARN

Distance: 7km/4.3mi; 2h35min

Grade: easy, with a short ascent/descent of 60m/200ft. You must be sure-footed. Green and yellow waymarking. *IGN map 2640 OT*

Equipment: see page 68; swimming things. Refreshments available at La Malène

How to get there: 🚗 to La Malène, halfway along the Gorges du Tarn (a detour on Car tour 8; see panel on page 50). No 🚌 service at time of writing; re-check at www.tourisme-aveyron.com or www.keolis-aveyron.com.

Alternative walk: La Malène — St-Chély. 10km/6.2mi; 3h30min. Grade as main walk. Follow the main walk to Hautrives, then continue along the riverside path to St-Chély, from where you can return to La Malène by taxi.

Stroll/picnic suggestion: Banks of the Tarn. Follow the walk to the 15min-point and back.

L a Malène, at the junction of roads connecting the Sauveterre and Méjean *causses,* was a focal point for the *transhumance* for centuries. Today it makes an ideal centre for exploring the Gorges du Tarn. Not only do the boat trips to the Cirque des Baumes leave from here, but it's the perfect spot from which to begin and end two splendid walks. This first ramble makes an superb early-morning or late-afternoon stroll to one of the prettiest hamlets in the area — Hauterives.

Start out at the CAR PARK in **La Malène**. Cross the BRIDGE (passing the TOURIST OFFICE on your left), and turn left on the D43 road to Meyrueis. After 30m/yds, turn left down a path marked with green and yellow flashes — the **Sentier de la Vallée du Tarn**. This is an exceptionally pretty stretch of the long-distance path, but it's *very* narrow in places (only about 30cm/12in), so *do* watch your footing. After passing some RAPIDS and just 30m/yds beyond a CONCRETE BRIDGE with an iron railing on one side, you come to a small GRASSY SHELF at the water's edge (**15min**) — an idyllic spot for a picnic.

About 800m/0.5mi short of Hauterives, the path gains 60m of height rapidly (some hand-

On the approach to Hauterives

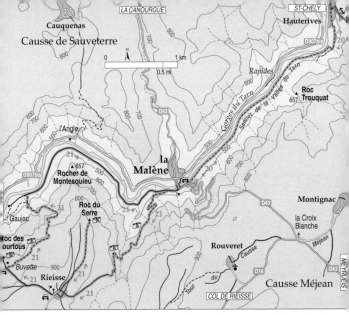

holds are necessary). Then it
descends again to **Hauterives**
(**1h20min**), one of several
beautifully-restored Causse-
nard hamlets along the banks
of the Tarn. The upper part of
the settlement (and the ruined
castle) can be reached by a path
just past the houses. But the
main walk turns back from the
riverside hamlet, retracing steps
to **La Malène** (**2h35min**).

Walk 21: ROC DES HOURTOUS

Distance: 9km/5.6mi; 3h50min

Grade: fairly strenuous, with ascents/descents of 500m/ 1640ft overall. Most of the paths are excellent, but the steep descent requires sure-footedness and can be very slippery when wet. Yellow waymarking. *IGN map 2640 OT*

Equipment: see page 68; refreshments available at La Malène, Rieisse and the seasonal *buvette* at the Roc des Hourtous

How to get there: 🚌 to La Malène (see page 126). No 🚐 service at time of writing; re-check at www.tourisme-aveyron.com or www.keolis-aveyron.com.

Short walks: both are easy; access by car: take the *difficult* hairpin road (D43) from La Malène towards MEYRUEIS. Turn right at a crossroads (La Croix Blanche) on the D16 and, beyond the Col de Rieisse, turn right again towards Rieisse village.

1 Roc du Serre. 35min return. Park at the junction with a cross, at the edge of Rieisse (sign: PANORAMA ROC DU SERRE). Follow the main walk from the 1h40min-point to the viewpoint and return the same way.

2 Roc des Hourtous. 30min return. Continue past Rieisse following PANORAMA DES HOURTOUS. Park near the *buvette* (open from May to October). Follow the main walk from the 2h35min-point to the 2h50min-point and return the same way.

The stupendous outlook to the north from the Roc des Hourtous, with the Tarn below and the Causse de Sauveterre opposite. This viewpoint is just above Les Détroits (not shown in the photograph), the narrowest part of the gorge, where the sheer cliffs rise 400m/1300ft from the river. It's hard to believe, but in the early 1990s a French tightrope walker had a 1km-long cable strung across the gorge from these cliffs. He crossed it on foot and returned on a motorbike, with his wife suspended in a basket!

One of the most spectacular walks in the Tarn, this is an ideal day's outing. Fortunately there is plenty of shade, so the walk is possible even at the height of summer. The views from the top are among the finest in the Tarn. The less energetic can see the best of the sights in the Short walks but, while it's easier on the legs and lungs, the drive up to Rieisse (via ten hairpin bends) is not for the faint-hearted!

Start out at the CAR PARK in **La Malène**. Cross the BRIDGE (passing the TOURIST OFFICE on your left), and turn right on a track (▪: ROC DES HOURTOUS). After 150m/yds, turn left up a path marked with yellow flashes. Although there is plenty of shady foliage, you will come to several viewpoints back over La Malène's setting as you climb. The path rises in easy zigzags, minimising the fairly tiring ascent of 450m/1475ft.

After a final pull to the top of the **Causse Méjean** you come into the village of **Rieisse**. Follow the waymarks up to a junction with a STONE CROSS dated 1739 (**1h40min**) and turn right (▪: PANORAMA ROC DU SERRE). Walk along the lane (closed to cars) and keep right at three Y-forks, always following the main grassy, later earthen track.

From the **Roc du Serre** (**2h**) you enjoy a plunging view back down over La Malène and

La Malène from the D43: the car park is still empty, but a tour coach is approaching, and the kayaks are at the ready behind the bridge.

the comings and goings along the river, over to the Causse de Sauveterre, and back to the *lacets* of the D43 snaking up to the Causse Méjean.

Return to the stone cross and now take the motorable track to the right (sign: *PANORAMA DES HOURTOUS*). The way-marked path turns off the track to pass to the right of the *buvette* at the **Roc des Hourtous** (**2h35min**), then edges the plateau. This entire stretch, with springy moss underfoot, is incredibly beautiful in spring — an 'Easter basket' of blue, purple and yellow flowers, including several species of orchids.

Although the mixed wood-lands are thick, there are several promontories with splendid outlooks. You are just east of Les Détroits, the narrowest part of the gorge. Looking back, your view encompasses the Cirque des Baumes and the Point Sublime in the west.

After 800m/0.5mi, watch for your left turn down a narrow footpath (**2h50min**) which demands careful footwork. Once back down at the RIVER-SIDE (**3h20min**), turn right and follow the track (**Sentier de la Vallée du Tarn**) back to **La Malène** (**3h50min**).

Walk 22: CHATEAU DE MALAVIEILLE AND LA LIEUDE

Distance: 10km/6.2mi; 3h10min

Grade: easy-moderate, with ascents/descents of 300m/1000ft overall. Some agility is required at the château. Good surfaces underfoot, but *no shade*. Unreliable waymarking, if any at all. *IGN map 2643 OT*

Equipment: see page 68; refreshments available at nearby Octon and Salasc, or from the *buvette* at La Lieude (July-Aug *only*)

How to get there: 🚗 to Malavieille (Car tour 9, page 52). Turn right on the first tarred lane west of Malavieille (after 0.4km) and park on the left immediately (rough 'parking' sign). No 🚌 service nearby at time of writing; you can check at www.herault-transport.fr.

Short walk: Le Castelas. 1.6km/1mi; 50min. Grade as main walk (ascent/descent 150m/500ft). Park 2km past

Malavieille, at a large open shelter and the path up to the ruined château (*castelas*).

This beautiful walk is also interesting from a geological point of view. We cross a landscape of *ruffes* and climb a 'thimble' of basalt, recalling the volcanic origins of the area. Embedded in this burgundy-red soil are fossilized animal prints dating from the Permian Period.

Looking south along the Rieupeyre Valley to the silhouette of the Château de Malavieille in the middle distance. This area, near Lake Salagou, is famous for its ruffes — *furrows of clay-bearing limestone soil. The striking contrast between the green grass and this red soil is one of the highlights of the walk in spring and early summer.*

Anti-clockwise from above: the old farm of Villetelle may be abandoned, but is definitely not for sale!; cacti near Le Molinas; don't miss the little chapel of St-Pierre near Mérifons; view north to La Lieude and the Château de Malavieille

Start out at the PARKING AREA: walk north along the tarred lane (*no waymarks*). Past a long cactus hedge, by the hamlet of Le Molinas, the route forks. Go half left, past wood and metal sculptures and a yurt or two, following the wide earthen track into a little valley. You soon come to the 15th-century **Chapelle St-Fulcran** (**15min**), dedicated to Lodève's patron saint.

Three minutes past St-Fulcran the track makes a U-bend to the left; keep straight on/right, following the electricity wires. An old stone-laid trail comes underfoot, as you mount the flanks of the **Montagne de la Boutine**. Climbing in deep zigzags, you enjoy fine views of the plain below, especially the vineyards in the southwest (where the photograph on page 52 was taken). **Pradels (40min)** is a huddle of honey-coloured stone houses. Leave the hamlet on a narrow concrete lane, continuing along the mountainside. Soon you enjoy the view shown on page 131: you look straight down the deep **Rieupeyre Valley** to the silhouette of the *castelas* (Château de Malavieille) on the far side. In spring the lime-green hillsides are ablaze with bright yellow broom.

The highest point of the walk is soon reached (spot height 431m; **1h**). From here you look out right to Le Mas Bas and Brenas, rising from a patchwork quilt of fields. Just past this point, turn left at a T-junction and descend due south towards the *castelas* on another lane (a right turn leads to Le Mas Bas). The concrete gives way to a delightful two-wheel track. Look to your left now: on the far side of the Rieupeyre Valley, wine-red *ruffes* stream vertically down the hillsides through the broom like lava flows. When you pass a BARN on the right (**1h20min**) and come upon a cultivated field, walk along the left-hand edge of the field and then curve round to the right. Now locate the *very clear* earthen path to the ruins, on your left (be sure to find it, or you will end up lacerated by brambles). From the ruined 12th-/13th-century *castelas* (**Château de Malavieille; 1h35min**), enjoy the panorama with your picnic.

On the very steep, stony descent watch for old waymarks indicating the best footholds. You descend to a SHELTER housing fossilised imprints of *Thereapsides*, precursors of mammals. They lived in this area, where there is thought to have been a watering-hole, some 250 million years ago (long before the dinosaurs). They were probably furry and warm-blooded.

With your back to the shelter, head right along the road to **La Lieude (2h05min)**. Pass the last house on the left (a *buvette* in summer) and its nearby shed, then immediately turn left down a faint path. This becomes a clear earthen path and crosses the **Salagou Stream**. Go ahead on a two-wheeled track, crossing another bridge a minute later. A short climb follows: bear left at a fork. From here there is a good view towards Lake Salagou and back to the ruins and the Rieupeyre Valley. Turn left at a T-junction (the abandoned **Villetelle** farm is on the right). At the next fork go right uphill, heading between fields towards some cypresses.

On reaching **Le Mas Canet (2h45min)** turn left. At an intersection, where there is a CROSS on the right, continue straight on. Meet the D8: turn left towards BRENAS/OCTON but, after 200m/yds, go right on a narrow tarmac lane (the first one you come to). Not long after crossing a CONCRETE FORD you reach **Malavieille** and turn left back to the PARKING AREA (**3h10min**).

Walk 23: CIRQUE DE MOUREZE AND MONTAGNE DE LIAUSSON

See also photograph on page 174
Distance: 5.5km/3.4mi; 2h35min
Grade: easy-moderate, with an initial climb of 300m/1000ft. The paths in the *cirque* are very stony underfoot. *You must be agile*. Little shade en route. Green, then blue waymarking. *IGN map 2643 OT*
Equipment: see page 68;

refreshments available in Mourèze
How to get there: 🚍 to Mourèze (Car tour 9). No 🚐 service nearby at time of writing; you can check at www.herault-transport.fr.
Short walk: Cirque de Mourèze. 1h. Grade as main walk, but ups and downs of about 100m/330ft. Follow the red-waymarked route.

Not only does this walk explore the extraordinary Cirque de Mourèze from all angles, but from the Montagne de Liausson you enjoy the best possible view over Hérault's famous beauty spot, the Lac du Salagou.

Begin the walk on the main road in **Mourèze**, just east of the CHURCH; follow ☛ DIRECTION DU CIRQUE along a lane. Turn left towards the church at the first alley, and then turn right. Past the last house, at a fork, ignore the left-hand path to the Col des Portes (your return route). Keep straight ahead to an INFORMATION BOARD showing the way-marked routes.

We'll follow the green route to the Col des Portes, then the blue. Head towards the right of the large PILLARS OF ROCK straight in front of you. *The Short walk (red route) goes left in front of these pillars; follow the three other colours to the right here, also keeping close watch for OLD, DARK BLUE DOT WAYMARKS.* The main path runs in a ROCKY CLEFT (**10min**) just below and to the right of these pillars. *Watch the waymarks.* About 100m/yds or so short of the Sphinx (the rock formation shown on page 174), follow waymarks to the left — into another narrow cleft in the rock, below and just to the left of the **Sphinx** (**15min**).

Eventually the path veers to the right, edging towards Mount Liausson. When you come to a T-junction (spot height 317m; **35min**), ignore the blue- and yellow-waymarked path to the right; turn *left* on the green route. The path is fairly steep, but not very stony, and it is pleasantly shaded by holm oaks. If it's still there, *ignore* the word 'Danger' and the 'X' on a rock on the path; it is someone's idea of a joke... You gain height quickly and easily, at the same time enjoying ever-improving views to the south over Mourèze and its *cirque,* the Pic de Vissou (with the transmitter), and the distant sea. Caroux and the Espinouse rise in the west.

Just after crossing an old charcoal-burners' circle, you reach the SUMMIT RIDGE of the **Montagne de Liausson** (**1h15min**) and the viewpoint shown opposite, with the Causse du Larzac and the Cévennes in the distance. From here head west along the grassy crest. You pass to the right of the ruined priory of **St-Jean d'Aureillan** and then reach a

134

Above: Liausson and the Lac du Salagou from the summit of Mount Liausson; right: church at Mourèze

CAIRNED SUMMIT (535m; **1h 30min**). This is a fine view-point over the dolomitic pillars in the *cirque* and the Nougarède Valley beyond Mourèze. The descent to the Col des Portes begins here. At a fork 12 minutes downhill be sure to go right; the path down to the left leads to some more inter-esting dolomitic formations, but is a cul-de-sac.

At the **Col des Portes** (**1h50min**) the green route goes straight on and the yellow route goes right. We turn left down a wide track, following a *pale blue arrow* (⬆: MOUREZE). Under 15 minutes down from the col, *be sure to turn left* on a path (pale blue arrow). The blue route brings you back into the *cirque* just north of the ruined CASTLE. Huge rock pillars soon tower above you, as you battle your way through a tall forest of pungent broom. Back at the fork first encountered at the start of the walk (**2h25min**), turn right, pass the CHURCH, and return to the road in **Mourèze** (**2h35min**).

Walk 24: GORGES D'HERIC

Distance: 11km/6.8mi; 4h
Grade: moderate-strenuous, with ascents/descents of 500m/1640ft overall (400m/1310ft at the outset). Excellent surfaces underfoot. Unreliable old waymarking except for the red/white GR halfway through the walk. *IGN map 2543 OT*

Equipment: see page 68; refreshments available at Mons and halfway through the walk, at Héric

How to get there: 🚌 to Mons, above Mons la Trivalle (Car tour 9); park near the church. Or 🚌 482 or 450 to Mons La Trivalle (www.herault-transport.fr), from where you must climb to Mons (0.8km/0.5mi; 15min each way).

Shorter walks: Both start at the PARKING AREA for the Gorges d'Héric, well sign-posted from the D908 at **Mons-la-Trivalle.**
1 Gouffre du Cerisier. 3.5km/2.2mi; 1h05min. Easy ascent/descent of 150m/500ft. Follow the concrete lane in the gorge from the parking area to the lovely pool and waterfall, just before the third bridge. Return the same way.
2 Héric. 9km/5.6mi; 2h50min. Moderate ascent/descent of 300m/1000ft. Follow the concrete lane in the gorge from the parking area to the isolated mountain hamlet of Héric (refreshments). Return the same way.

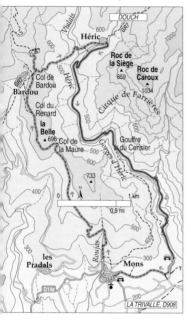

Whether you only do the short stroll up to the Gouffre du Cerisier or you huff and puff up to Héric via the Col de Bardou, you can anticipate a glorious and rewarding day out. Your physical needs are catered for with plenty of shade and beautifully-surfaced paths underfoot. Spiritually the walk is as fulfilling as a symphony, with lofty peaks piercing the clouds above you, an emerald-green river bouncing down beside you, and the trill of bird-song.

Start out at the CHURCH in **Mons.** Climb the narrow alley just opposite it, heading up towards an arch (*faded* BLUE/WHITE FLASHES on an electricity pole on the left). Walk under the ARCH and turn left in front

of the *gîte*, into another alley. Curve round to the right, uphill, on a concrete lane (Rue de la Croix), passing a CROSS on the left. At the Y-fork here, keep right uphill (Rue du la Costete). When you reach a

136

SHED/GARAGE straight in front of you (**5min**), turn right, between houses. (If the owners of the houses have scattered some belongings across the path, don't worry that you have stumbled into a private garden; just forge ahead.) At the far edge of the house on the left, turn left up steps, to begin climbing an old stone-laid trail. There is a *faded* BLUE FLASH on the wall at the left and an improvised arrow sign on the right, 'GGR7 [sic] VERS HERIC/BARDOU' — as well a large BLUE MOSAIC TILE SALA-MANDER on the wall! A minute

This bridge over the Vialais (a tributary of the Héric) is an ideal swimming and picnicking spot.

Top: Héric, below the Espinouse massif; left: the large swimming hole at the Gouffre du Cerisier, fed by a waterfall

along, when the trail forks, go left.

When the trail crosses the bed of the **Ruisseau de Roujas** (**25-30min**), you may notice some blue paint waymarks enticing you up the bouldery stream bed. *Ignore them.* Keep left, following the faded BLUE TRIANGLES AND RED FLASHES. The reason for the superb stone-laid trail is soon apparent: myriad walls and a broad-leafed canopy overhead testify to intensive cultivation of the chestnut tree in the past. If you come in early summer, when the berries have fallen to the ground and lie squashed in pools of black juice, you'll also notice the mulberry trees, with their oval, serrated leaves. Mulberry trees were introduced (especially around Ganges) as early as the 13th century, to develop the silkworm industry; the caterpillars fed on mulberry leaves.

A huge CAIRN on the right announces the **Col de la Maure** (**1h05min**). Continue uphill, in 10 minutes passing to the left of another large CAIRN. When you reach a fork at the **Col du Reynard** (**1h30min**) *keep right,* even though you may spot blue triangle and red flash waymarks directing you down to the left. Follow the path with an old BLUE 'X' on a tree. (The waymarks lead down to Bardou, but we pass *above* the hamlet.)

When the GR7 path comes up from behind on the left (from Bardou; **1h40min**), keep ahead, almost immediately coming to the **Col de Bardou**. Here a stony path goes ahead uphill and the GR, our ongoing route, turns down to the right beneath more chestnuts. Before taking it, follow the path ahead for a few minutes, then climb over bedrock to the iron railings. From this superb viewpoint you look out to a prominent 'hoof'-shaped double peak higher up the valley, over towards Héric and down along the gorge.

Returning to the Col de Bardou (**1h55min**), now follow the GR quite steeply downhill. You cross the **Vialais Stream** on the bridge shown on page 135 (**2h20min**). At a fork almost immediately after the bridge, turn left uphill, past another stream. Soon signposts announce the *buvette* at **Héric** (**2h35min**) and our ongoing route (towards DOUCH). Handily, the path leads straight through the outdoor terrace of the café. So stop awhile, under the flowering ash, the fig, or the false acacia.

Then continue to the concrete track on the far side of the terrace and turn right downhill (the GR7 climbs a path to the left here, to continue to Douch). Some 25 minutes downhill, you look straight up ahead at a needle of rock called **La Belle**; the Col de la Maure, where you encountered the first big cairn, is just to left of it. Further down, the jagged, green-tinged peaks of the **Cirque de Farrières** ahead seem to cut off our ongoing route, but the track bends round and crosses a FIRST BRIDGE (**3h**). Beyond a SECOND BRIDGE we come to the **Gouffre du Cerisier** (**3h05min**), where a large pool on the right is fed by a lovely waterfall. A THIRD BRIDGE is crossed just below an impressive escarpment much favoured by rock-climbers. Beyond a FOURTH BRIDGE (**3h25min**) we leave the gorge. Ignore the road down left into the car park (where the Shorter walks begin and end): keep straight ahead for two minutes, then turn sharp right uphill on a concrete path (passing a *gîte* called **Le Caroux** on your right). The path skirts to the right of a VINEYARD. Where a track comes up from the left, turn right uphill on a wider path, still beside vineyards on your left. In 15 minutes, where a path comes in from behind to the right, keep ahead (left). Under five minutes later, at another T-junction amidst the houses of **Mons**, turn left downhill to the road*, then go right, back to the CHURCH (**4h**).

---

*Just before press date, red/yellow GRP waymarking had appeared at the junction of this street (Rue du Caladou) and the main road, but we did not have time to check the route, so have not added it to the map.

Walk 25: CIRCUIT ABOVE OLARGUES

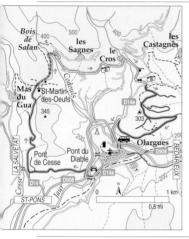

See also photograph page 53
Distance: 9km/5.6mi; 2h30min
Grade: fairly easy, with an initial ascent of 150m/500ft. Good surfaces underfoot. No waymarking, but easily found. *IGN maps 2543 OT*
Equipment: see page 68; refreshments available at Olargues
How to get there: 🚗 to Olargues. Park in the car park by the river, at the *western end* of the village, by the 'Centre Cebenna' (Car tour 9). Or 🚌 482 or 450 to Olargues (www.herault-transport.fr).

This walk in the foothills of the Monts de l'Espinouse is both easy and rewarding. There are several fine viewpoints en route, but other corners of interest as well, like the delightful chapel of 'St Martin of the Eggs' shown overleaf. At the end of the walk you might like to climb the 11th-century bell tower, for its fine panorama, unimpeded by trees.

The walk begins at the CAR PARK in **Olargues**. Just to the north, the ancient **Pont du Diable** (1202) spans the Jaur. Cross the MODERN BRIDGE leading to the D908 and turn right. Then take the first left turn uphill — a narrow concrete road on the far side of a defunct service station. You rise in a westerly direction up to the little **Cesse Valley**. You may spot some ancient blue and white waymarks here, but they are very faded, so follow the notes carefully!

The road dips and you come to a T-junction (**20min**), where there is a POST BOX ahead. Go uphill to the right here, in the direction of Caroux above the Gorges d'Héric (setting for Walk 24). The concrete gives way to track, and soon you're climbing past some of the abundant cherry trees that characterise this walk (in late

May it's torture not to pick them). At a Y-fork (**40min**), go right uphill. Five minutes later you are just opposite the village of Mas du Gua. The bare rock edges of the Espinouse massif rise above you here, but it is always to the high rock escarpment beyond the Gorges d'Héric that the eye is drawn. In another minute, when you come to a fork, go left. The tiny chapel of **St-Martin-des-Oeufs** (**53min**) on the right bears the date 1889.

Just past this chapel, ignore trails to the left and straight ahead; turn right, then take the *upper* grassy trail through a lovely chestnut wood, the **Bois de Salan**, passing above a stone hut after about 40m/yds. Two minutes past the chapel, at a Y-fork, bear right down into the **Combe des Codouls**. Foxgloves brighten this shady bower in early summer. A small BRIDGE is crossed and, two minutes later, you meet the little road from Les Sagnes: turn right downhill. Ignore roads and tracks coming in from the right, and eventually enjoy a fine view towards the bell tower on its wooded knoll. Notice how some of the red roof tiles in **Le Cros** (**1h22min**) are weighted down with stones as a protection against the *mistral*. This largish hamlet boasts a marvellous view eastwards along the valleys of the Jaur and Orb. Two minutes later, at the sign denoting the entrance to the hamlet, don't go straight ahead

View east to the priory of St-Julien on the descent back towards Olargues. On the right are the long valleys of the Jaur and the Orb.

The walls of St-Martin-des-Oeufs are decorated with charming frescoes.

past the village wash house; curl downhill in a U-turn to the left, into a pretty glen, and cross a BRIDGE over a healthy stream.

Three minutes later keep right at a fork, immediately passing to the right of a modern barn built in traditional style. After another three minutes (some 300m/yds beyond the bridge; **1h30min**), you come to a road junction: turn right downhill, passing to the right of two traditional stone barns. Straight ahead now, on the far side of vineyards, is the **Prieuré de St-Julien**.

Just as the road completes a U-bend to the right, go left uphill on a concrete track (tarred at the outset), passing to the right of a BARN. The triangular peak to the left, at the far end of the valley is Tantajo, near Bédarieux. Follow the concrete track in a U-bend to the right, ignoring a farm track off left (**1h41min**). Four minutes later, at a three-way fork, keep ahead on the middle track. From here there is a splendid view up to Caroux and along to where Tantajo punctuates the end of the

valley. Pass below a barn up to the right and, at the three-way junction that comes up a minute later, ignore the tracks straight ahead and to the right: go left downhill, following the electricity wires on your right. Just after passing a plantation of firs, the priory seems within arm's reach.

Go right at the next fork, after five minutes noticing a cypress-studded CEMETERY below on the left and walking straight towards the bell tower. Olive trees border this stretch of track. When you meet the the D14e (**2h10min**), turn left downhill. Cross the D908 and the bridge over the Jaur. Walk left uphill towards CENTRE VILLE, then take the first lane up right into **Olargues**. Stroll southwest, back to the CAR PARK (**2h30min**).

Walk 26: CIRCUIT ABOVE ST-PONS

Distance: 9km/5.6mi; 2h40min
Grade: moderate, with ascents/descents of 300m/1000ft overall. Good paths and tracks, but the descent into St-Pons is quite steep and stony. At press date waymarking was sparse or non-existent: pay careful attention to the text! Ample shade. *IGN map 2444 ET*
Equipment: see page 68; refreshments available at St-Pons
How to get there: 🚌 to St-Pons. Park in the shady Place Forail, on the D907 just north of the roundabout (Car tours 9, 10). Or 🚌 214, 482 or 450 to St-Pons (www.herault-transport.fr); also 🚌 953 (Castres–Béziers line; www.transports.midi pyrenees.fr). Or 🚆 to St-Pons (www.ter-sncf.com)

Short walk: D907 above Brassac to St-Pons. 4.5km/2.8mi; 1h30min. Easy, but a short, steep descent into St-Pons. Access with friends or taxi to the starting point: drive north on the D907 towards *LA SALVETAT.* Just under 1km past the turn-off left for Brassac, watch for two stone pillars on the right with a sign, '*LA BORIO DE ROQUE*'. Start here by picking up the main walk at the 1h10min-point.

H ere's a lovely and varied ramble, ideal for a morning or afternoon. You start out along a burbling stream and climb — mostly in shade — to the foothills of the Somail massif. Picking up the old 'road' from La Salvetat to St-Pons, you stride out across a grassy ridge — drenched in yellow broom in spring or purple heather in summer and autumn.

We first did this walk decades ago; it was suggested by the superb tourist office in St-Pons. They are no long promoting the route, and it was only partly waymarked as we went to press, but if you follow the notes carefully you should have no problems with route-finding.

Start out at the **Place Forail**, where there is a roundabout at the junction of the D907 and D612. (The tourist office and the headquarters of the Haut-Languedoc Regional Park are also located here, in separate buildings.) Walk north on the D907. Where the road curves right (by a sign advising whether the Col du Cabarétou is open), go straight ahead across the BRIDGE. Continue to the right up a tarred road, with the hexagonal façade of a large medical building on your left and the SCULPTURE PARK on your right.
At a fork (**5min**), keep straight uphill for HOPITAL. When the road goes left (**6min**), head right on the **Traverse de Semmen**. At a Y-fork (**7min**) go left. Ignore a tarred road up left to houses; keep ahead on a shady track (**9min**).
You pass the farm of **St-Mens** on the far side of the stream and then a tarmac lane comes in from a bridge on your right; keep ahead now, on the lane. Beyond a house (**Les Foulons**) you cross a bouncing STREAM. When the lane turns right uphill to another house, keep ahead on a narrower track (you may spot old waymarks on the pole at the left of this track).

143

The track ends at two buildings (**Cabrol**; **25min**). The path passes just to the right of the buildings and continues uphill as a shady earthen footpath. A STREAM runs about 4m/12ft over to your right. The path eventually curves left, away from the stream, and emerges on a track (**40min**). Turn right here. After 250m/yds this track makes a hairpin bend to the right. Go straight ahead on a lesser track. Meeting a fork almost at once, keep right; then ignore a track to the right. You pass to the right of a HUT. Four minutes later you come

to the D169 (**50min**). Walk left downhill, past a sign for **Brassac** village. After 120m you pass a concrete farm building on the right and then a concrete electrcity pole. Your ongoing footpath is on the right, just 10m/yds past this pole: it starts out in a stream bed (sometimes quite wet). But before moving on, take the time to spot your first (and maybe last!) waymarks of the day: if you walk a few paces *past* your path and turn round, you'll see red/yellow flashes on the roadside — intended for people coming the other way.

On the descent back to St-Pons, with the cathedral in view

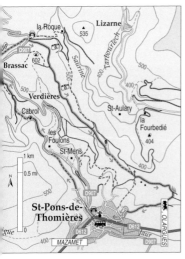

This beautiful path* quickly rises out of the stream bed and climbs gently to the D907 (**1h10min**). Cross the road to a sign, *LA BORIO DE ROQUE*. Ignore the track between the two stone pillars here, but climb the grassy track at the right of it. *(The Short walk begins here.)* Within 10 minutes you clear the chestnuts and find yourselves on top of a ridge. Here the track bends right, but keep ahead on a lesser track, heading southeast on what was once the old road between La Salvetat and St-Pons. The hamlet of Lizarne is seen to the left across the valley, while the farm of La Fourbedié lies below, set like a gem in the midst of tree-darkened slopes. Below it you may notice the remains of the priory of St-Aulary. A flower-bedecked *KNOLL* (**1h30min**) affords fine views to St-Pons. *Note the town's*

*At press date this path had just been made part of the Haut-Languedoc GRP network stretching between St-Pons and Lunas near Lodève. Perhaps eventually the rest of the walk described here will be included and waymarked.

position and from this point on follow the text *and map* carefully, keeping to the crest of the ridge as you continue southeast.

When a track comes in from the right (**1h45min**), keep left. Then, about 15m/yds further on, take the first right, down a grassy track (there may be an old sign to St-Pons here). Ignore a track off right some 75m further on. Walk round a barrier seen up ahead, then pass to the right of a tall shooting hide that would not be out of place in a WWII prisoner-of-war film.

Eventually the track narrows to a shady path. Descend below chestnuts, walk under *POWER LINES*, then continue down under holm oaks and pass to the left of a *HUT*. A path comes in from the left behind you, you pass an *IRON CROSS* on the left, and come immediately to a T-junction (**2h05min**). Turn left (to the right is a short-cut to St-Pons).

In three minutes you pass two large *STONE HUTS* *(capitelles)* on the right; you are now on a jeep track. At a fork by a *CYPRESS HEDGE* on the left (**2h15min**), go right downhill. A minute later, at a T-junction, turn right. When you meet a T-junction with a concreted lane (**2h 30min**), go left (**Chemin de Cousteau**). At the next T-junction, go left and then immediately right, on **Rue de Cousteau**. Pass to the right of the well-restored *MARKET* and meet the D612. Turn right past the lovely *HOTEL DE VILLE* (left) and the *CATHEDRAL* (right) to the **Place Forail** (**2h40min**).

Walk 27: GORGES DE L'ARNETTE AND HAUTPOUL

Distance: 9km/5.6mi; 3h40min

Grade: moderate, with ascents/descents of 360m/ 1180ft overall. Good surfaces underfoot, but some stretches can be slippery in wet conditions. Green and white PR, red and white GR way-marking. *IGN map 2344 ET*

Equipment: see page 68; refreshments available at Hautpoul

How to get there: 🚗 to Moulin Maurel (Car tours 9, 10). Park by the roadside. Or 🚌 951 from Castres to Mazamet (www.midipyrenees. fr); click on 'Transports'. Or 🚆 (www. ter-sncf.com) to Mazamet (follow lilac lines on the map to join the walk just north of St-Sauveur chapel).

Longer walk: Moulin Maurel — St-Pierre-d'Esplos — Hautpoul — Brettes — Moulin Maurel. 16km/10mi; 5h20min. Fairly strenuous, with ascents/descents of 500m/ 1640ft overall. From Moulin Maurel walk south along the D54 past the junction with the ROAD TO PIC DE NORE. Some 150m/yds past this junction you approach a STONE WALL on the right. Leave the road just *before* this wall, taking the clear footpath on your right, descending straight into the gorge. *Take care* on this path (you only follow it for a minute or two, but it is very narrow, and the drop to the right is precipitous). The path takes you to a BRIDGE. Cross the **Arnette River** and then climb a narrow tarmac lane. When you come to a fork, ignore the grassy trail ahead; go left, to climb above a large mill down on the road. Pass a stream to the right, go through a makeshift gate, then climb

146

through chestnuts, oaks, and beech. On reaching a farm (**Les Cousteilles; 50min**), curl up right between the buildings and leave the farm, passing a large GARAGE/BARN on right. Ignore the grassy track off to the right just past the farm; keep straight ahead uphill on a lane. Then ignore another grassy track into a field; keep climbing under aromatic pines. When you come to the drab chapel of **St-Pierre-d'Esplos** (**1h**) on the left, with its large cemetery, curve right on the road, leaving the chapel off to your left. After 200m/yds, by a CONCRETE CROSS, fork right up a slight incline (▐: HAUTPOUL, MAZAMET). Come to another fork, where there is an IRON CROSS: go right. Your route is now a signposted *Sentier bota-nique* (and the GR7). Start the descent, with fields sweeping away to the left. When you come to a three-way fork (about five minutes downhill), ignore the track off left into fields *and* the motorable track straight ahead; take the middle track (half-left downhill). In a minute or so *again* take the middle fork. This is still the *Sentier botanique*, but it's as stony as a river bed. Soon a well-placed bench overlooks a valley leading into the Arnette. Beyond the bench, at a T-junction, head left downhill. When you come to a crossing track, go straight over and downhill on a footpath. Two minutes later (by a shed on the right with a *Chasse Privée* sign), continue straight ahead on a track, to a junction with a tarmac road, where you turn right downhill, to **Hautpoul** (**1h40min**). Now pick up the main walk at the 55min-point and follow it to the end.

The ancient fortified village of Hautpoul, a Cathar stronghold (see panel on page 62) destroyed in 1212, and the bounding Arnette River are the highlights of this circuit — a fascinating introduction to the ecclesiastical and industrial history of the Montagne Noire.

Start out at the signpost for the hamlet of **Moulin Maurel**. Cross the **Arnette River** on the more southerly of the two bridges (by the village sign), pass a *WASH HOUSE* on the right and, after a garage on the right, go right up a steep tarred lane. This reduces to steps and then a narrow shady path. You rise quickly, with fine views over the Arnette. Beyond a stile, at a T-junction with a path, turn right, soon passing an arrow pointing to *HAUTPOUL*. The red roofs of the Arnette factories shine up through the trees, and the river gurgles noisily below on the right. 'Waterfalls' of grass spill down the banks of this luxuriant path.

When Hautpoul becomes visible up to the left, *ignore* a path to the left and come to a road. Cross it and, just opposite, take steps down towards the river. Now on a cobbled trail, you pass a humourous wooden sculpture on the left and come onto a gravel track. At the right is a *RESTORED MILL*, now an artisans' workshop for wooden toys. On the left is the **Arboretum d'Hautpoul** (**30min**), a delightful place for a picnic. From here the track contours above the river to a junction by a *WEIR* and a *MILL IN RUINS*. Take the track to the left, then leave it immediately, heading half-left on a path (↑: *HAUTPOUL, GR WAYMARKS*).

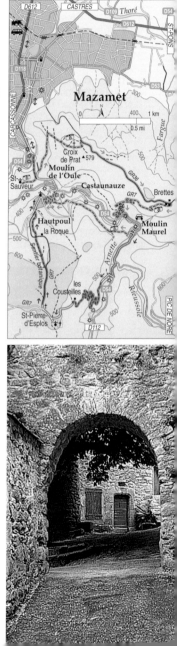

Alley in Hautpoul

Before long, cobbles come underfoot: this is the old salt route between Narbonne and the Montagne Noire. The deep zigzags minimise the ascent to **Hautpoul (55min)**, where a statue of the Virgin rises on the site of the old castle, destroyed by Simon de Montfort after a seige lasting four days. Wander through the archways and past the old façades and beautiful doorways. A balcony view-point overlooks the houses snuggled below the Virgin's rock and the Arnette Valley — from where you can hear the delightful sound of rushing water.

After your visit, return the way you came, being sure not to miss the overgrown ruins of the Romanesque church of St-Pierre (straight ahead as you descend past a shop on the left selling wooden toys and drinks). Go through an arch at the end of the village, then turn left down steps leading back into the old salt route.

Following the GR waymarks, you pass a tiny CEMETERY on the right.

Back at the junction by the RUINED MILL (**1h30min**, having allowed 15 minutes to walk around Hautpoul), cross the river and meet the D54 at **Moulin de l'Oule**. Now climb the tarmac lane opposite (more GR and green and white waymarks). About 200m/yds uphill, just after passing a few houses, fork left on a signposted footpath to the ruins of **St-Sauveur** (**1h45min**), the Cathar church which fell along with the rest of Hautpoul in 1212. It looks out south to the Virgin on the far side of the Arnette and north to Mazamet.

Returning from St-Sauveur, as you approach the lane, ignore the steps half-left (⌐: GR36, MAZAMET). *(But those travelling by bus or train will use this lower part of the old salt route to get to the main walk.)* Continue on the lane (⌐: CROIX DE PRAT). Then, about 50m/yds past the

Left: view over Mazamet and the surrounding countryside from the Croix de Prat; below: the old salt trail

Old mills in the Arnette Valley. In the 18th century the nascent textile industry was cradled here, and wool was washed in the river. With the coming of the machine age, the industry grew so rapidly that a new town had to be built — Mazamet. But the Arnette was still critical to its success: its waters now supplied the necessary electricity.

path to the chapel, fork right uphill on a dirt track. This narrows to a path through a mixed wood — mostly chestnut. As it traverses northeast, *watch carefully* for your turn-off sharp right after about 800m/0.5mi *(if you come to a Y-fork, and the path is descending, you have gone too far)*. Turn up sharp right, cross another path, and begin the *real* climb. Keep right at a Y-fork 20 minutes up and go straight over a large junction a minute later. At the next Y-fork, the paths rejoin. It's a steep climb to the **Croix de Prat** (**2h30min**), but the view of Hautpoul, Mazamet and the north is magnificent.

From the cross the green and white waymarks point left, but we take the path straight ahead, at the *right* of the cross (not waymarked). It rises to a T-of paths, where you turn left downhill. In five minutes you emerge on a track and turn right (GR36, green and while waymarks). Now ignore any paths or tracks off this well-waymarked track. Passing under oaks you come to the farm of **Brettes** (**3h**), where you join the GR7. Follow waymarks to circle round the buildings, onto a footpath at the right of a field. The gorgeous Arnette Valley opens up below you, all too briefly. Coming into a forest, zigzag downhill through holly and conifers on a beautiful old trail. You drop down to the D54 by a large WORKING MILL, where wool is washed and defatted (**3h30min**). Turn left to follow the road beside the river, back to flower-filled **Moulin Maurel** (**3h40min**).

Walk 28: CANAL DU MIDI — CARCASSONNE TO TREBES

See also photographs pages 54, 56-58 and cover
Distance: 14km/8.7mi; 4h10min
Grade: very easy. Red and white GR waymarking at the start, then no waymarking. *IGN map 2345 E*
Equipment: see page 68; no refreshments available between Carcassonne and Trèbes
How to get there: 🚗 to La Cité (Porte Narbonnaise; Car tours 9-11). Or 🚌 (see www.carcassonne.org or www.

teissier.fr/horaires) or 🚌 955 (www.midipyrenees. fr). Or 🚃 (www.ter-sncf.com) to Carcassonne, from where you can start the walk at the bridge over the Aude. Return by 🚌 10 (www.carcassonne.org), 🚃 or taxi from Trèbes
Short walk: Trèbes — Ecluse de Villedubert — Trèbes. 8km/5mi; 2h. 🚗 (Car tour 10; park near the canal) or 🚌 10 or 🚃 (websites above) to Trèbes. Walk to the Villedubert Lock and back.

The Canal du Midi, one of the most evocative images of the south of France, was created by the ingenuity of one man and the labour of 12,000. Among the obstacles to be overcome was a 174m/570ft-high ridge west of Carcassonne. Paul Riquel, a wealthy tax collector, had the solution: bring in water for the locks from the rushing streams of the Montagne Noire. He even put up a third of the money himself, sacrificing his daughters' dowries. Sadly, he died in 1680 — six

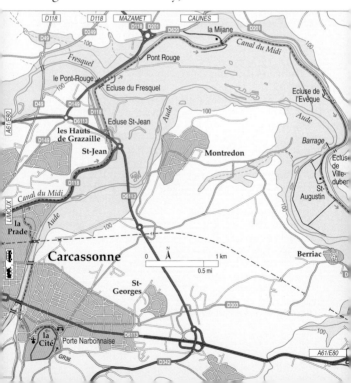

The canal can be utterly tranquil (see pages 56-57) — or bustling with activity.

months before the canal was opened. With the building of the adjacent Canal Latéral à la Garonne in the 19th century, the link to the Atlantic was complete, fulfilling a dream dating back to Roman times.

Start out at the **Porte Narbonnaise**, the main gate to **La Cité**. With your back to the gate, walk left downhill on the road (GR36), keeping the large CAR PARK on your right. In two minutes fork left up a path (GR waymark on a lamp post), to skirt the walls of the citadel. Two minutes later come to a tarmac lane and go left uphill into a square. Walk to the front of the church (**St-Gimer**), cross the road to the *boulangerie*, and turn right. Go straight over a crossroads; you approach a BRIDGE and a PARK. Cross another road and go through the park. Turn right under the bridge in the park (**Pont Vieux**) and then head left down to the track beside the Aude. Turn right on the track and walk under the main D6113 road bridge (**Pont Neuf**). Continue to the next BRIDGE (**30min**) and turn left to cross it. On the far side, swing right, back down to the river. Walk under the RAILWAY BRIDGE, beyond which the path curves left uphill. Cross a lane and go straight up a road (GR

The fairy-tale towers of La Cité in early spring (see also pages 54, 58).

waymark on a lamp post on the right). You climb through a housing estate (**La Prade**); at the first opportunity, turn up right to the main road (D118; you will hear the traffic). Cross the road, drop down to the TOWPATH (**45min**), and turn right. For the next few hours you will amble beside this delightful waterway, cheering on the rented holiday barges as they navigate the short elliptical locks.

At at the **Ecluse St-Jean** (**1h 05min**), you part company with the GR. Continuing to the echo of bird song, you reach a bridge at **La Mijane** (**1h50min**). At the **Ecluse de Villedubert** (**3h10min**), Ville-dubert can be seen across the lock, shaded by palm trees and cypresses. Here you have to leave the canal, but keep along a track going in the same direction; the Aude, and a weir, are just on your right.

Continue ahead, at the left-hand side of a quarry, on a track running above the canal. In five minutes you pass the houses of **St-Augustin** and five minutes later rejoin the canal.

On coming into **Trèbes**, where there are picnic tables on the far side of the canal, you approach a bridge. Don't cross it; turn right in front of it, following CARCASSONNE. Soon you will pass a BAR on your right (**4h10min**), where you can have a drink and telephone for a taxi. Or, to get to the railway station and bus stops, cross the Aude and continue along the D610 for another 0.5km/10 minutes. (A circular walk, returning along the Aude, would have been ideal, but is not possible; there is nowhere to cross the river between Trèbes and Carcassonne.)

152

Walk 29: MINERVE

Distance: 5km/3mi; 2h
Grade: fairly easy ascents/descents of 200m/650ft overall; agility required in some places. *Sparse yellow waymarking. No shade. IGN map 2444 ET*
Equipment: see page 68; refreshments available in Minerve
How to get there: 🚌 to Minerve. From St-Pons-de-Thomières (Car tour 10) take the D907 south for 25km, then turn right on the D10e and right again on the D10, following MINERVE. Park on the D10 just before the village (paid car park). No 🚐 access at time of writing, but check www.teissier.fr and click on 'Les Lignes Régulières', to see if a new line has been introduced.

The site of Minerve, astride a rock buttress at the confluence of the Brian and Cesse gorges, has been inhabited since prehistoric times. Its fame, however, derives from one of the most brutal battles in the Albigensian wars (see panel on page 62): in 1210 Simon de Montfort laid seige for seven weeks until his catapults destroyed the Cathars' water supply and the people were forced to capitulate. They were given the choice of surrender or death; 180 chose death by pyre.

Start the walk at the CAR PARK on the D10. Cross the bridge into **Minerve** and walk to the top of the village. Head left towards the spiky tower of the old château. Walk to the right of the tower, then descend a stone-laid path on the right (just past a small vegetable garden; there is a GR 'X' on this path). The path curls down into the **Brian Gorge**, then levels out and turns back to the right (south), to circle below the village (the '**Chemin de Ronde**'; **15min**; YELLOW WAYMARKS). As it again curls right to head southwest, you'll see a replica of *La Malvoisine* on the far side of the gorge — the most feared of all de Montfort's catapults, as it was just across the gorge from the water supply. Cross the footbridge on the left now, just at the confluence of the **Brian** and **Cesse**. Then take steep steps up the far side to a cart track, the **Chemin de l'Estrade**. Turn left here, passing to the right of *La Malvoisine*. The views from this plateau, into the Brian Gorge and over to Minerve, are superb.

La Malvoisine, *a replica of the catapult responsible for the destruction of Minerve's water supply in 1210*

At a THREE-WAY FORK (**30min**), take the cart track back to the left, ignoring the track ahead (your return route) and a path to the right. You skirt the edge of the cliffs above the Brian, with good views back to the Chemin de Ronde. There are vineyards on the right, and you will follow these to the top of the climb. When a cart track comes in from half-right, keep ahead towards a house. Pass just to the left of the house (**La Courounelle; 1h02min**) and keep ahead on the surfaced lane. At a fork two minutes later, keep right on the lane (YELLOW FLASH). From here there is a good view down over

The Brian Gorge

the Cesse Valley and La Caumette. Ignore a track coming in from the left in two minutes; walk ahead on the surfaced lane (YELLOW FLASH on a telephone pole).

You pass to the left of the few houses of **Padene** (**1h15min**). The small Goury Gorge is on your left and vineyards on the right. Keep to the lane, rising through **Mayranne**. At the exit from this hamlet, don't go downhill left on the road, take the gravelly track straight ahead, rising slightly. When the way levels out, ignore a track off right to a farm and then a cart track off right. You can see the D10 down to the left, on the far side of the Cesse.

When the track meets another, wide track (perhaps a fire-break) on a bend (**1h32min**), turn right. But after just 25m/yds, descend half-left on a minor cart track *(no waymarks)*. Minerve is on your left now. The track descends quickly to an abandoned vineyard (overgrown with bright-blooming wild flowers in spring). Walk round or across the field, then make a U-turn to head back the way you came, so that Minerve is on your *right* and *La Malvoisine* is ahead of you. Making straight for the catapult, you come onto a track at the edge of cultivated vineyards: follow it straight ahead, back to the three-way fork first encountered at the 30min-point.

Back at *La Malvoisine* (**1h 40min**), retrace your steps to cross the FOOTBRIDGE (noticing some enticing grassy paths down to the Brian as you go) and rise back to the **Chemin de Ronde**. Turn left to

continue the circuit, passing the covered walkway leading to the Cathars' water supply (**Chemin Couvert**) and the well itself (**Puits de St-Rustique**). The Chemin de Ronde continues as a track running just above the **river Cesse**, past caves. Ignore steps up right to the Poterne Sud (the south keep) and continue

straight ahead on asphalt. On the left, just before the modern road bridge, is one of two rock tunnels (PONT NATUREL), where the Cesse carved its way through the limestone (in summer, when the water is low, you can walk through it). Pass the road down to the cemetery and head up the road towards the village. At the T-junction turn sharp right, cross the bridge, and return to the CAR PARK (**2h**).

Walk 30: CIRCUIT ABOVE LAGRASSE

How to get there: 🚗 (Car tour 11) or 🚌 (www.teissier.fr/horaires) to Lagrasse

Short walk: Montagne de la Côte. 3.5km/2.2mi; 1h40min. Fairly easy, with ascents/descents of 210m/670ft overall. Follow the main walk to the 1h10min-point. Turn right here, just *before* the notice board, then turn right again. After 200m/yds, go half left on a path between stone walls (large cairn on the left), soon passing a *borie* on the right. You rise 50m/165ft and *keep left*, to cross the crest of this mini-mountain. Descend on an old trail, ignoring the path that comes in on the right after 400m/yds (from the Pied de Charlemagne). Meet a track and turn right, picking up the main walk again at the 2h15min-point.

Distance: 6km/3.7mi; 2h25min

Grade: fairly easy ascent/descent of 160m/525ft. Yellow PR waymarking. *IGN map 2446 O*

Equipment: see page 68; refreshments in Lagrasse

There is some evidence that the Abbey of Lagrasse was founded in 799 by the Emperor Charlemagne. True or not, the area abounds with place names referring to him. While the 'high point' of the walk — literally and figuratively — is the view from the Roc de Cagalière, you will also come across 'Charlemagne's Foot' and look out to 'Charlemagne's Buttocks'!

Lagrasse from the Roc Cagalière. Les Fesses de Charlemagne (see panel opposite) are visible on the hillside to the left of the abbey tower.

Le Pied de Charlemagne: according to legend, this is the hoof-print of Charlemagne's horse. The emperor was returning from a successful campaign against the Saracens when his mount made a false step. Despite his undoubted horse-manship, the emperor was flung clear across the valley, where his ample buttocks (fesses) left their imprint on the hillside (the rounded green slopes with an indentation of scree down the middle in the photograph opposite).

Start out at the SCHOOL on the main D3 in **Lagrasse**, walking south towards RIBAUTE. Pass the D212 to Ribaute on the left, and 50m/yds further on turn left up a concrete lane (☞ on the left: SENTIER D'EMILIE, LE PIED DE CHARLEMAGNE, then ☞ on the right with a map of the route). Ignore all turn-offs as you rise, with a fine view back to the abbey. Just past a HEDGE OF CYPRESS TREES on the left, at a three-way junction, take the middle route. Three minutes later, just after this eroded track completes a U-bend to the right and begins to curve left, turn left up a footpath (**20min**; waymark and CAIRN). This lovely path — the old trail between Lagrasse and Tournissan — rises gently northeast through pines towards the Roc de Cagalière. At a Y-fork, turn left, passing a small field on the right. A path takes you the short way up to the top of the **Roc de Cagalière** (**40min**), the perfect viewpoint down over Lagrasse, north to the Montagne d'Alaric, and south over the rolling hills of the Corbières. If the wind is in the right direction, the Pyrenees will emerge from the haze. Return from this rock promon-tory the way you came, with the little field now on your left. Back at the fork beyond it, turn sharp left. When you meet a forestry track, turn left and follow it round a hairpin bend to the right, contouring through pines. While there are no views now, this track on the eastern flanks of the miniature **Montagne de la Côte** is a delight of wild flowers in spring. Some 600m/yds along the track, watch on the right for a path marked with two CAIRNS and follow it 50m/yds (past a ruin on the right) to another, small rock outcrop with a large circular hole — the **Pied de Charlemagne** (**50min**; photograph above). There is a path from here directly down to Lagrasse, but we haven't tried it.

Return to the forestry track and continue to the right. As a track comes in from behind you to the left (from Ribaute), you come to a junction with a GREEN WATER TANK and WALKERS' INFORMATION PANEL (both on the right; **1h10min**). *(The Short walk turns right here.)* Walk past the tank and, after 30m/yds, turn left on the **Sentier botanique** and follow its meanderings until you

157

Bord Rouge is a most attractive vineyard just below the Col Rouch, on the D3 to Tournissan.

regain the forestry track further south. The colour of the track underfoot changes to deep iron-rich red soil and you reach the **Col Rouch** (Red Pass; **1h35min**). (Another legend has is that the soil is stained red with the blood of martyred Cathars.) Ignore the track straight ahead here; curve to the right, then turn right off the main track (quickly passing a : *SENTIER PEDESTRE*). From this track there is a superb view down left over the vineyards of

La Peyrouse and north towards Lagrasse and the abbey, with Charlemagne's Buttocks above to the left and Alaric rising in the background. Ignore both a cairned path on the right (**2h15min**; the Short walk descent) and, just over 150m/yds further on, the path you ascended at the start. Retracing your outward route, you come back to the SCHOOL in **Lagrasse** (**2h25min**).

Walk 31: CIRCUIT ABOVE TERMES

See also photograph page 63
Distance: 8km/5mi; 2h45min
Grade: easy-moderate, with ascents/descents of about 300m/1000ft overall; ample shade. Red and white GR, faded yellow PR waymarking. *IGN map 2447 OT*
Equipment: see page 68; refreshments: *buvette* in Termes, or Lagrasse (12km)
How to get there: 🚗 to Termes (Car tour 11); park at the roadside near the entrance

to the château (there is also a car park further east). No 🚌 access
Short walks/picnic suggestions: 1 Watercourse. Up to 50min. Easy; follow the main walk to the 15min- or 25min-point and back.
2 Serre Laitière. 1h15min. Easy ascent/descent of 160m/525ft. Walk to the château and continue uphill past it, to Serre Laitière.

W ithout doubt our favourite walk in the Corbières, this ramble is extremely varied and beautiful. You start out along a gurgling watercourse, climb to a flower-filled plateau and descend past an idyllic farm to the Château de Termes and then to the enchanting village itself.

Start out in **Termes** by crossing the bridge to the château. On the far side, turn left on the CAMIN DEL MOLIN, beside the **river Sou**. After passing behind the *MAIRIE*, you pick up red and white GR waymarks. You're following an old watercourse that used to

supply the mill. Cross a grassy track and continue straight ahead. Then turn right in front of a fenced-in vegetable plot; after a 10-15 paces you meet a much wider watercourse, which you follow to the left, with the murmuring river not far below. The play of light and

View back to the Château de Termes on the descent into the village at the end of the walk

shade is delightful on this stretch.

A *DAM* (**15min**) marks the start of the waterway. Walk back a few paces from the dam, then turn left up a clear path. It rises quite steeply away from a meander in the river, then drops again; soon the river is jumping down in tiers beside you — a beautiful spot (**25min**). Just over five minutes later the path finally leaves the river, heading southwest through an open grassy area. At a fork some three minutes along, igore the path to the right; continue straight ahead. But at the Y-fork which follows immediately, go right (where the other branch goes down to the river). At this point you may notice a distinctive rock pillar ahead — the **Roc de Femme Prenz** (Pregnant Woman). We've reached the bed of the **Nougairole Stream** (**35min**): hop across it (there's little water) and continue on the

Above: dam at the source of the watercourse that once fed the mill at Termes but is now used for irrigation. Left: Roc de Femme Prenz (Pregnant Woman Rock), one of the landmarks on the walk

path on the far side, climbing towards the Roc de Femme Prenz through the **Forêt Domaniale de Termes**, a mixed woodland where oak and beech predominate. Watch for a path on your left and turn downhill to a *VIEWPOINT* (**1h**)

The pastoral landscape of the Bergerie de Serre Laitière

over the **Sou Gorge** and the waterfall that feeds it.

Then return to the main path which quickly crosses a natural rock 'bridge' (**Pont de la Caune**) above an enormous CAVE on the right. Although this section is very narrow (about 1.5m/4ft wide), it is just 4m/12ft long and would only be potentially dangerous in *very* strong winds.

As you contour now at the foot of the **Nitable Roc** buttress, there are open views due south to the table-topped Montagne de Tauch with its relay. The path dips, then quickly rises to

the TOP OF THE PLATEAU (**1h25min**). In case of mist, *watch carefully for the GR and faded PR waymarks here*, but on clear days the main path through the flower-filled *garrigues* is easily seen. Up here you're on top of the world, with open views to the Pech de Bugarach and the Pyrenees.

Descending from the plateau, the path heads northwest, with the Caulière Valley below to the left. *Again, watch for waymarks carefully on this stretch*, as the path zigzags (at the first of these *lacets,* a path contours ahead, but you must turn *sharply back to the left.*) About five minutes after entering a beautiful oak wood, *again take care:* at a fork, where the GR goes sharp left, keep *straight ahead* on a contouring path (faded YELLOW FLASH). Ten minutes later come to the idyllic **Bergerie de Serre Laitière** (**2h10min**), from where you follow a contouring track to the foot of the **Château de Termes** (**2h35min**). Continue down to **Termes** (**2h45min**).

Walk 32: PEYREPERTUSE AND THE FONTAINE DE LA JACQUETTE

See also photograph on page 62

Distance: 4.5km/2.8mi; 2h15min

Grade: strenuous ascent/ descent of 330m/1100ft; ample shade. The paths are very slippery when wet. You must be sure-footed and have a head for heights. Yellow PR, red and white GR way-marking. *IGN map 2447 OT*

Equipment: see page 68; walking stick(s). Refreshments available at nearby Rouffiac

How to get there: 🚗 to the Col de Grès (Car tour 11).

Note that there is no sign on the D14 identifying this col: locate it from the map below. Two tracks, 50m/yds apart, head south from this col. The sign for the col is at the start of the most westerly track. Alternatively, start in Rouffiac: follow the GR36 (see map). No 🚌 service

Short walk: Fontaine de la Jacquette. 2.5km/1.6mi; 1h20min. Quite strenuous ascent/descent of 150m/490ft, requiring agility. Follow the main walk for 40 minutes, then jump to the 1h35min-point.

The most famous and extensive of the Cathar châteaux, Peyrepertuse makes for a short but fairly demanding hike. From the site, it seems the world is at your feet. Later in the walk, the rock chaos below the Fontaine de la Jacquette is a veritable rock garden of wild flowers, moss and holm oaks.

Start out by following the westernmost track at the **Col de Grès** (small ☞: COL DE GRES, FONTAINE DE LA JACQUETTE). In three minutes the grassy track bends 90° left and narrows to a path. From here on *watch your waymarks;* there are many twists and turns as the path dips slightly, then begins its steady ascent through pines (**8min**). The only unmarked stretch comes up about 30 minutes uphill (four minutes past a small scree), when the path bends sharp right and rises over a low wall: only after the path bends left again will you find a yellow waymark on a tree.

When you meet the CROSSING GR (**40min**), which has taken a different route up from the col, turn right and follow the red and white waymarks another 145m/475ft uphill, to the **Château de Peyrepertuse** (**1h10min**). From here the views are magnificent — you look over the Verdouble Valley to Quéribus and Tauch, to Bugarach and the Pyrenees. If you decide to visit the fortress (see footnote on page 61), it will cost you the entrance fee plus another 60m/200ft of ascent to the Château St-Georges (not included in the main walk).

Return to the JUNCTION WITH THE PR ROUTE (**1h35min**) and turn right. The path falls steeply to the 13th-century

Fontaine de la Jacquette. It was probably built in the 13th century by St-Louis. His mother lost her silver goblet there.

Fontaine de la Jacquette (**1h45min**), built when the Peyrepertuse fortifications were being extended.
Beyond here the path drops through a mixed wood and moss-coated rock chaos, crossing a few rock screes. Cairns as well as waymarks guide you on this enchanting but demanding stretch.
Beyond the final, long scree (a rock garden of wild flowers), *watch out:* the path bends sharp left.
After you pass a SPRING on the left (**2h05min**) the way widens to a track and descends gently to the **Col de Grès** (in the last 20m/yds joining the GR; **2h15min**). Turn left, back to your car.

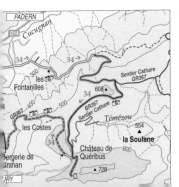

Walk 33: CIRCUIT BELOW PEYREPERTUSE

See also photograph page 62
Distance: 4.5km/2.8mi;
2h15min
Grade: easy, with two short
ascents (150m/500ft overall).
Some of the paths are narrow;
some are stony. *Little shade.*
Outside summer, when the
river is high, it may not be
possible to reach the waterfalls

shown below. Yellow PR way-
marking. *IGN map 2447 OT*
Equipment: see page 68;
refreshments available in
Duilhac
How to get there: 🚗 to
Duilhac-sous-Peyrepertuse
(Car tour 11). Park on the
D14 near the *auberge* and
hostellerie. No 🚌 service

This walk below Peyrepertuse looks up to the
château from the south — not the best vantage
point. But the best part of the walk in any case is the
'marble' river bed of the Verdouble, with its tiered
waterfalls.

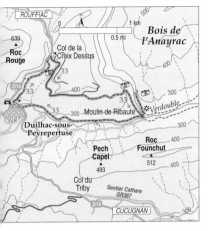

stony path at first *seems* to descend, it really climbs up to the left in a tight U-bend, and then descends into the valley. Now the **Verdouble Gorge** opens up on the left, and from the vertiginous edge of the path, you will have the tremendous view shown opposite. On reaching a T-junction with a stony track (**1h**), *go left* (ignoring any yellow 'X'). You come to a concrete embankment at the river's edge. On the far side is the the ruined **Moulin de Ribaute**, an old wheat-grinding mill. If you do this walk in high summer, it's likely that you'll find planks in place, allowing you to cross the river here. If not, you should at least be able to cross a ford a short way downstream, to reach the mill and the cascades.

From the river return to the junction at the 1h-point and go straight ahead. The track soon narrows to a path. Walk to the right of a first vineyard and then go left, to keep a second vineyard on your right. This shady path is a flutter of butterflies. Watch your footing, however; it is narrow in places, with a hefty drop. Having climbed back to the D14 in **Duilhac** (**2h15min**), turn right, back to the *auberge* and *hostellerie*.

Start out on the D14 in **Duilhac**: from the *auberge* and *hostellerie* walk southeast (towards Quéribus) for about 100m/yds, then turn left down a narrow lane below the village; there's a sign for the walk at the right. (If you come to the *boulangerie*, you have gone too far.) You'll soon see yellow flashes. Leaving the gardens behind, the waymarks take you beside a vineyard. Now on a footpath, you walk below and parallel with the road; Peyrepertuse rises above you to the left.

The path rises steeply up to the D14, where you turn right and follow the road for 35m/yds, to the **Col de la Croix Dessus** (**35min**). Go right here on a cart track, following the electricity wires (☞: MOULIN DE RIBAUTE). Now there are fine views back to Duilhac, with Peyrepertuse above it. At a U-bend, leave the track and follow the footpath ahead for about 15 minutes, enjoying some glimpses of the vineyards in the Verdouble Valley through foliage. When the

Left: the turquoise waters of the tiered cascade in the Verdouble

Walk 34: CIRCUIT TO QUERIBUS

See also photograph page 60
Distance: 8.5km/5.3mi; 3h
Grade: moderate, with an ascent/descent of 340m/1115ft. The descent path is very steep in places and requires agility. *No shade;* on sunny days, start out early, when there is some shade from the cliffs. Yellow PR, red/white GR/Sentier Cathare way-marking. *IGN map 2447 OT*
Equipment: see page 68; walking stick(s). Refreshments available at Cucugnan
How to get there: 🚍 to the most easterly entrance to Cucugnan off the D14, 0.65km east of the tourist office (Car tour 11). Park beside the road, near the sign: CENTRE VILLE. No 🚐 service

While the holocaust at Montségur is generally regarded as the last battle in the crusade against the Albigensians (see panel on page 62), Quéribus continued to provide refuge for a handful of Cathars. In 1255 St-Louis eradicated this final pocket of resistance, but it appears that the castle was taken by trickery, not by armed assault. At that time Quéribus stood on the border between France and Aragon, so its capture greatly strengthened the line of royal fortresses guarding the frontier. Only in 1659, when the border was moved further south, did Quéribus lose its strategic importance.

At the eastern entrance to Cucugnan there is a sign, CENTRE VILLE, to indicate that motorists should continue along the D14 to the western entrance for best access to the village centre. **Start the walk** opposite this sign. Walk southwest down the lane between two small vineyards: an electricity pole at the left has both yellow and GR waymarks, and there is usually some sign around here indicating horse riding.

After 100m/yds you pass a lane off right with a signpost indicating CHATEAU DE QUERIBUS and red/white flash waymarks (the return route). On the left there is an attractive stone FOUNTAIN. Keep straight ahead here, following yellow and orange flashes on a post. At a Y-fork 100m/yds further on,

keep left. Walking between vineyards, you cross a stream and go straight ahead on the lane. 350m/yds further on, keep right at two Y-forks in

Cucugnan

succession, eventually passing a stand of cypresses at **Les Fontainilles** (**20min**). The lane curls back west for a short time (affording a fine view back over Cucugnan and to Peyrepertuse and Bugarach), before resuming its easterly traverse towards the flat Montagne de Tauch with its relay.

When the tar ends at a fork (**45min**), turn half-right up a bulldozed track. Now you have to make your way up this extremely unpleasant track for the next 35 minutes, until you reach a contouring track on the crest. This is the **Sentier Cathare/GR367** (**1h20min**), which runs from the Château d'Aguilar to Peyrepertuse, and is waymarked with the usual red and white flashes. Soon you have a first view of Quéribus, with the Pyrenees (hopefully snow-capped) behind it. A beautiful ridge is ahead too, rising on the south side of the Cucugnan Valley — the Roque de la Pourcatière. Behind it, to the right, is the silhouette of Bugarach.

From the PARKING AREA for the **Château de Quéribus** (**1h45min**; ticket office, WCs, picnic tables), a path rises another 100m/300ft to the château itself — add 1h return, should you decide to visit it.

Château de Quéribus

The main walk continues by turning right uphill to where the Quéribus access road/parking area ends (red/white GR flashes, ⌐: CUCUGNAN, DESCENTE DIFFICILE). This is where the most beautiful (if most demanding) part of the walk begins: *take it slowly*. Your ongoing path rises through *maquis* aglow with tiny blue grass lilies *(Aphyllanthes monspeliensis)* to a grassy promontory, dips, rises again and then descends *very* steeply down the shoulder of **Les Costes** (keep right at a Y-fork a short way down). The views — back to Quéribus and the Pyrenees, over to Peyrepertuse, the Roque de la Pourcatière and Bugarach, and down to the Cucugnan and Verdouble valleys are magnificent. Once down in the valley (**2h**

30min) the path contours through high grass. At a T-junction with a track, go right. The **Bergerie de Granan** is set up on the left. Making straight for Cucugnan, pass to the right of a house. Some 15 minutes along the track, ignore a track off left and then a track off right.

Now walking on a level track between vineyards, you look up right to the cliff you rounded earlier and the ridge traversed by the Sentier Cathare. You quickly meet the bend of a tarred lane: turn left, then follow the lane in a curve to the right (ignoring another lane off to the left). The lane curls right, back towards Tauch (where a cross is visible) and emerges on the lane where the walk began. Turn left, back to the sign CENTRE VILLE (**3h**).

Walk 35: CIRCUIT ABOVE TUCHAN

Distance: 6km/3.7mi; 2h25min
Grade: moderate, with ascents and descents of 300m/980ft overall; *little shade*. You must be agile: the descent path from the chapel is slippery when wet and it may be a problem to cross the Ruisseau de Faste outside summer. Since this stream crossing is near the *end* of the walk, you may prefer to start at the chapel: if so, from Tuchan take the little road above the wine cooperative signposted to MONT TAUCH and (perhaps also) NOTRE-DAME-DE-FASTE, and begin at the 1h35min-point — to tackle the stream crossing first. Yellow PR waymarking. *IGN map 2447 OT*
Equipment: see page 68; long trousers, walking stick(s).

Refreshments available at nearby Tuchan (5km)
How to get there: 🚗 to Ségure (detour on Car tour 11). From Padern drive to Tuchan and, in the centre of the village, take the D39 signposted to MAISONS and PALAIRAC. No 🚌 service

The Château of Ségure and the chapel of Notre-Dame-de-Faste are the highlights of this gorgeous walk in the foothills of the Montagne de Tauch, but you'll also see an overgrown old hamlet and … an angora goat farm!

Start out at the pretty hamlet of **Ségure**: take the cart track just south of the houses and little bridge (🏁: NOTRE-DAME-DE-FASTE, YELLOW ARROW). You're heading towards the Montagne de Tauch. Turn right on another track (**5min**; waymarked), and then go sharp left immediately. At a fork two minutes later (where there is a solitary house on the left), go steeply left uphill on a narrow eroded path. The path bends 90° left, above the house, and levels out amidst a plethora of *Lavandula stoechas* and white Montpellier *Cistus*. Tauch, with its transmitter and wind generators, is on your left now, and you can see the chapel of Notre-Dame-de-

Faste above. Soon the castle, your first goal, comes into view on the right, and you approach it on a grassy path through typical maquis.
When you come onto a cart track, follow it to the right, to a grassy area with cypresses. Three tracks are ahead: ignore the gravel track to the left (your ongoing route) and the track to the right (to a house belonging to the 'Château de Ségure' vineyards). Take the grassy track straight ahead, then go left on a footpath, to rise to the ruins of the **Château de Ségure** (**25min**), a lovely picnic spot.
Return from the château and turn hard right on the gravel track (with the sign CHATEAU

169

Left: you pass a house belonging to the Ségure vineyards, then approach the ruined château via an arch. Below: angora goats at the Mohair du Tauch

downhill to the chapel of **Notre-Dame-de-Faste (1h 35min)**. Legend has it that the chapel was founded by sailors in peril, who were only saved by seeing a light atop the Montagne de Tauch, although the ceremonial use of the site, with its nearby spring, probably dates back to pagan times. (Water is available at the picnic area 150m down the access road).

To return to Ségure, walk to the right of the main door, then turn right down a steep path at the east end of the chapel. *Watch the waymarks carefully throughout the zigzag descent.* When you approach the **Ruisseau de Faste (1h 45min)** you may find that the footbridges are washed away. If so, you'll have to scramble 1.5m/4ft down into a messy, muddy gully and over to the right-hand side of the stream. Two minutes later you have to repeat the exercise, to get back to the left-hand side (where the path ahead is marked with an 'X'): this is best done by heading a short way left upstream, where the drop is less (again 1.5m/4ft).

After regaining the left-hand side of the stream, a VINEYARD will be on your right. At a T-junction with a motorable track (**2h05min**) turn right, then follow it in a curve to the left, ignoring the minor track on the right. You walk between vineyards, then just beside the right-hand side of the river. Reaching the D39, turn left for 350m/yds, back to **Ségure (2h25min)**.

DE SEGURE on your right). Follow this downhill below the ruins but, after only 50 paces, turn hard left on a path, descending below the cypresses in the parking area. At a fork 15 minutes along, keep right on a track and, two minutes later, at a Y-fork, go right on an eroded path. Strawberry trees enliven this stretch, but it is a hefty climb and very tiring in heat. Finally the path levels out in a grassy area amidst a myriad of wild flowers.

At a farm (*LE MOHAIR DU TAUCH;* **1h25min**), where you'll see long-haired angora goats, you come to a gravel track. Enjoying a fine view back to the ruined castle and over vineyards, follow the track

Walk 36: THE 'ROMAN' BRIDGE AT BUGARACH

Distance: 4.5km/2.8mi; 1h40min

Grade: easy-moderate, with ascents/descents of 130m/425ft overall, but agility is required; some of the paths are steep and narrow, slippery when wet. Yellow PR waymarks. *IGN map 2347 OT*

Equipment: see page 68; refreshments available in Bugarach

How to get there: 🚗 to Bugarach (Car tour 11); park near the Mairie. No 🚐 service

Short walk/picnic suggestion: Pont Romain (2km/1.2mi; 30min). Park by the transformer on the D14, just over 2km west of Bugarach village. Follow the walk from the 32min-point to the bridge and return the same way.

Alternative walk: Pech de Bugarach. 6km/3.7mi; 3h. Strenuous ascent/descent of 560m/1850ft. You must be sure-footed and have a head for heights (only recommended for *very* experienced walkers). *Do not attempt the ascent after rain, and be prepared for very strong winds between the col and summit.* The path begins at the Col du Linas, on the D14 east of Bugarach village.

Autumn 1992 brought terrible storms to south-western France. Swollen rivers swept away several Roman bridges (including the single-arched span at Vaison-la-Romaine). The people of Bugarach lost their Roman bridge too, but the following year local stonemasons donated their time and talents to create an exact replica. Yet however pretty the little gorge and the new 'Roman' bridge, the superb views over to Bugarach provide the highlight of this walk.

Start out facing the *MAIRIE* on the D14 in **Bugarach**. Turn right down a track on the west side of the building (↑: *SENTIER DU PONT ROMAIN*). After crossing a little bridge, walk to the left of a cinder-brick wall on a farm track. Bugarach rises to the left, while you cross the grassy fields surrounding Bugarach village. When the track curves right, there is an especially fine view to the peak. On coming to the D14 again (**20min**), follow it to the left for 1km/0.6mi, until you come to an electricity *TRANSFORMER*. Turn right here, through an old gravel quarry (**32min**; ↑: *PONT ROMAIN*). At a Y-fork, where the main track goes left, keep ahead on a grassy track. A *CATTLE ENCLOSURE* is on the left. The way narrows to a path

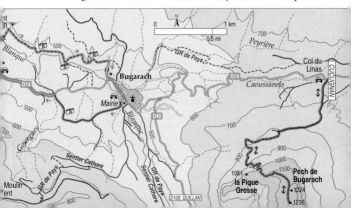

*Bugarach's new (1993) 'Roman'
bridge over the Blanque Stream*

and turns left, still beside the enclosure.

You rejoin the main track just at the start of the descent: turn right. In five minutes you're down at the new '**Pont Romain**' (**45min**), where a plaque pays tribute to the eight stonemasons who recreated the original bridge. The setting, a tiny gorge along the **Blanque Stream**, with rock pools and an old stone-laid path, is exquisite.

To continue the walk, climb the steep footpath to the right. At a T-junction (**50min**), turn right (◄: BUGARACH). (The way to the left is another way-marked walk, to La Vialasse). Through the clearings in the *garrigues* there are wonderful views down to the right over the Blanque Valley and east to Bugarach.

At a CLEARING from where you have the *best* view of the

mountain (**1h05min**), be sure to turn steeply left downhill (where the main path *appears* to go straight on). Steps cut into the rock help you down this eroded, fairly narrow path. *Watch the waymarking — there are several zigzags!*

The path climbs again, heading north via a couple of *lacets* to the left, where you may need to use hands and feet for short stretches. Finally, at the top of the climb (**1h25min**) you clear the trees and look down over the fields at the start of the walk and ahead to the Bugarach.

Coming on to an old stony track a couple of minutes later, you enjoy pretty glimpses of Bugarach village as you descend. Pass by a few houses, then follow a lane over a bridge, past a house on the left and to a WALKERS' INFORMATION BOARD by the D14 road showing all the hikes in the area (**1h35min**). Turn left on the road, back to the MAIRIE in **Bugarach** (**1h40min**).

The Pech de Bugarac, surrounded by a collar of grassy fields, is the focal point on this walk. The highest peak in the Corbières, this monolith of intriguing rock forms is best appreciated from the west, near Bugarach village.

Glossary

Bartizan: overhanging, battlemented corner turret (of a castle)

Baume: shelter beneath rock

Belvédère: elevated viewpoint

Bergerie: shelter for animals (and shepherds)

Borie: small drystone building, usually with a domed roof (photo page 79)

Buvette: snack bar

Camelle: pile of salt near salt pans

Capitelle: as borie

Castelas, castellas, castellaras: old ruined castle (photograph page 132)

Cathars: See panel on page 62.

Causse: vast limestone plateau, where most rainfall quickly seeps through the porous rock

Chasse privée: private hunting ground

Cirque: a valley ending in a deep rounded 'amphitheatre' of rock (photograph pages 48-49)

Cité: old term used for a grouping of citizens (as Lavène, Walk 16); also the oldest part of a city (as La Cité at Carcassonne)

Clos: enclosed parcel of cultivated land (photograph page 40)

Col: pass

Dégustation: wine-tasting

Dolmen: prehistoric sepulchral chamber of standing stones supporting a flattish stone 'roof'

Dolomitic rock: rock composed of soluble calcium and less soluble magnesium. The calcium erodes more quickly under the action of rainwater and streams, giving rise to weird formations, for which the French have a very apt name (*ruiniform;* see overleaf).

Domaine: estate (vineyard)

Garrigue, maquis: terrain resulting from the degradation of the Mediterranean forest (through fires or grazing), differentiated by the nature of their soil and characteristic flora. The *garrigue* is an open limestone wasteland on non-acidic soil, with small pockets of vegetation. Typical plants include Aleppo pines, kermes oak, holm oak, box, thistles, gorse, rough grass and wild aromatic plants like lavender, thyme and rosemary. The *maquis* is a dense covering of evergreen plants growing on acidic soil, usually with small hairy or leathery leaves to help withstand the dry conditions. Flora include trees like cork and holm oaks, junipers, box, strawberry trees and myrtle, as well as smaller bushes like rosemary, Jerusalem sage, broom, heather, and *Cistus.* Larger trees like chestnuts and maritime pines may also be present.

Garrigues, Les: an area north of Nîmes, described in Car tour 7, which exhibits the features of the *garrigue*

Gouffre: gulf, abyss

GR (Grande Randonnée): long-distance footpath, way-marked with red and white paint flashes; see page 70.

Grotte: cave

173

Lac Neuf, a lavogne near Lavène (Walk 16)

Lavogne: stone-paved basin for watering livestock

Manade: raising of bulls or horses in the Camargue

Maquis: see *Garrigue*

Maquis, The: French Resistance during World War II

Mas: country house, usually applied to a farm

Massif: mountain mass with various peaks

Menhir: ancient megalithic standing stone

Oppidum: defensive position of drystone walls at vantage points. The Ligurians built the first *oppida*.

PR (Petite Randonnée): local waymarked walk, fairly short, often circular; see page 70.

Resurgence: the reappearance above ground of a subterranean watercourse; for example, the Fontaine-de-Vaucluse (photograph page 28)

Rive droite, rive gauche: right bank, left bank of a river. (The banks of a river are defined *from* the source.)

Rocher: rock

Ruffes: eroded limestone slopes with a high red clay content, as at Salagou (photograph page 131)

Ruiniform: a chaos of dolomitic rock which has eroded into the shape of ruins. The rocks may look like a building or even a whole town, or sometimes a ruined sculpture. Montpellier-le-Vieux (Walk 19) and the Cirque de Mourèze (Walk 23, are textbook examples.

Sentier (botanique): footpath. (A *sentier botanique* is usually accompanied by information panels describing the botany and geology of a specific area; see, for example, Walk 5.)

Table d'orientation: panoramic viewpoint, usually with a circular stone 'table' marked with the points of the compass and pin-pointing the location of towns, mountains, etc.

Via: road. By 100BC Rome held much of the land between the Alps and the Pyrenees. Their most important highways were the *Via Agrippa* via Orange and Avignon to Arles, the *Via Aurelia* via Nice, Fréjus, Aix and Nîmes to Arles and then Spain (today the D6007/DN7 follows much the same route), and the *Via Domitia* via Sisteron, Apt and Pont Julien south to the *Via Aurelia*.

The Sphinx, a landmark in the ruiniform rock chaos at Mourèze (Walk 23)

● Restaurants

We only feature below places we visit regularly (including a couple of hotel stops on Car tour 8). *All* of these restaurants specialise in regional dishes. Since we often have the house wine, we've not gone into details of the wines, but most have decent wine lists. Prices range from € (inexpensive) to €€€ (fairly pricey) — don't be surprised to see €-€€€; you can have a relatively inexpensive meal in a top-class establishment if you choose just one course à la carte, the dish of the day, or the weekday *formule* — with house wine. Where specific prices are shown, they were correct at press date.

Aix-en-Provence
LA ROTONDE €-€€€
2A, Place Jeanne d'Arc (facing the Fontaine de la Rotonde at the start of the Cours Mirabeau), daily all year, 08.00-02.00; (04 42 91 61 70; www.larotonde-aix.com. No need to go into great detail here: their website tells you everything you want to know about ambience and food (although it is only in French at present). All we need say is: the location is marvellous, the staff extremely helpful and the dishes we had at last visit (risotto with gambas, foie gras sautéed with apples and port sauce) superb.

Arles
LE MALARTE €-€€€
2 Boulevard des Lices, daily all year (except Christmas) 08.00-18.00 (22.00 Mar-Sep); (04 90 96 03 99; www.le-malarte.com. This lively brasserie is right at the heart of the city, on a wide, plane-shaded avenue facing the tourist office and carrousel. There are *menus* at 12 €, 18 € and 24 €, as well as special offers on breakfasts, snacks and teas. Each of the 7 **entrées** is a meal in itself (like the risotto with Camargue crayfish, the escabèche of red mullet with aubergine tart, or the gourmande salad with duck breast and *foie gras*); there are **grills** (steak, fish, or fantastic tiger prawns in a mild curry sauce); **specialities** include bull

stew, duck tournados Rossini, lamb shanks Provençal, crusted sea bass, pan-fried skate with *pistou* butter. The assorted **cheeses** come with a salad; the **desserts** include crème brûlée with chestnut/rum preserve, warm biscuit with dark chocolate and cardamon ice cream, vanilla ice cream with olive oil from Nice and crushed almonds. We have had some *super* food here.

Aureille
LA TABLE DES ALPILLES €€-€€€
Place de l'Eglise, all year, cl Mon, also Wed and Sun dinner; (04 88 40 07 29; www.LaTabledes Alpilles.com. This has always been a favourite place to take a break between Walks 13 and 14, but it's a higher-class break these days! For the last year this pretty restaurant has been in the hands of Stephane Tougay, who trained at l'Oustau de Baumanière. As well as the exposed stone walls where the work of local artists is displayed, he has introduced out-door tables in the square for fine weather. The *carte* is purposely limited and concentrates on a marriage of Provençal and French specialities. The day we visited there were entrées of foie gras, gambas, escargots and goats cheese terrine; mains of fish, duck, lamb or veal; desserts like raspberry tartare with goats cheese or chocolate fondant with Tonka beans. Of course none of

175

this does justice to the preparation or presentation; you will be served a work of art. *And* there will be free hors d'oeuvres while you wait. A lunchtime visit Tue-Fri (not holidays) is ideal for the budget, with two *formules:* 15 € for two courses or 20 € for three! Other menus are priced at 33 € or (gourmet) 53 €. Our goujons of John Dory in saffron sauce, with pastry baskets of artichokes and pansies were luscious.

Avignon
LE FORUM €-€€
20 Place de l'Horloge, daily all year 08.00-01.00; ℂ 04 90 82 43 17; www.leforum-avignon. com. *Not* the best food in Avignon, but bright and breezy — ideal for people-watching, with a large terrace facing the town hall and theatre (glassed-in for winter). Popular with Avignon's 'ladies who lunch' and businessmen having the weekday **lunch** *formule* at 13 € (there are also 3-course menus at 19 € and 27 €). **Large** *carte* (which you can see on their website). In winter they usually offer several *choucroute* (sauerkraut) dishes as well — with pork knuckle, various Alsatian meats and champagne, even seafood!

Barbentane
LE ROMARIN €-€€
11 Avenue Bertherigues, all year 12.00-14.00 and 19.30-21.00, cl Mon, Tue lunch, Sun dinner; ℂ 04 90 95 58 43, http://romarin. eresto.net. Small, cosy, family-run restaurant, with Provençal-style tablecloths and decorated with old signs, pressed flowers and herbs. Daily *formules,* served at lunch *or* dinner, including at weekends: 14.00 € (choice of entrée + dish of the day or dish of the day + choice of sweet). Other *formules:* 'butcher's plate' (with a 400g steak, *frites* and salad) at 20.50 €; Romarin 'discovery' plate with seven

entrées from the main menu. Popular with the local people. **Plenty of choice** (see menus on their website; *not* up-to-date, but gives some idea of the range). Tasty food; *very friendly* service.

Baux-de-Provence, Les
AU PORTE MAGES €€
Rue Porte Mage (inside the village gate, just past the tourist office, on the left), daily all year (cl Mon from Nov until 11 Feb); ℂ 04 90 54 40 48. A real find — not only is this one of only a couple of year-round restaurants at Les Baux, but the food is *fantastic*. Stone walls, fireplace, colourful tablecloths inside (cosy in winter), lovely shady terrace for summer, very friendly service. Menus change seasonally; the summer menu is lighter — with more salads and puff pastry dishes. Daily **menu**: three courses 25 €. Enormous **à la carte** selection (5 pages!), featuring everything from **Provençal specialities** (bull steak, grilled lamb with herbs, tripe sausage, duck) to **puff pastries** filled with fish or meat; 8 different **salads** (with cheese, fish or meat); 15 savoury pancakes (*galettes,* made with buckwheat flour); for **dessert** 20 sweet pancakes, plenty of standard tarts and rich chocolate confections, 15 ice creams, 18 'gourmand' ice cream and liqueur combinations (try the pear sorbet drenched in pear liqueur!).

Buoux
AUBERGE DE LA LOUBE €€
Quartier de la Loube, limited opening times: Mon-Fri 20.00-21.30, also Tue/Wed/Fri/Sun 12.00-13.30; cl Jan/Feb; ℂ 04 90 74 19 58. Lunch *formule* at 26 € (not Sundays); dinner *menu* at 34 € (or 36 € including cheese). We first stumbled (literally) upon this restaurant in the course of researching Walk 4: we somehow managed to cross its terrace

at lunch time. There was no prayer of getting a table — the place was packed. *Book ahead!* The inn is famous for its **Provençal hors-d'œuvres** (16 € à la carte, a meal in itself). Served with warm bread, they are presented like Greek or Turkish *mezes* and may include include *anchoïade*, hard-boiled quails' eggs, *tapenade,* purées of aubergine and chick peas (Provençal houmous!), onion chutney, tuna, squid, beetroot, tomatoes, *brandade* of cod, asparagus and artichoke hearts in olive oil, peppers, lentils, melon, country hams, braised carrots with *aïoli*, asparagus in vinaigrette… Some people can then manage a main course of beautifully roasted lamb, followed by goats' cheese and salad and a cornucopia of sweets. Pleasant service, elegant, flower-filled dining room with large open fireplace — very welcoming in winter. But in fine weather, choose the terrace! Note that the Auberge des Séguins, where Walk 4 begins, has excellent reviews on several websites *and* apparently has a *buvette* open all day. Sadly, we've never had a chance to try it.

Carcassonne, La Cité
BISTRO FRUIT €-€€
6/7 Place Marcou, La Cité, daily all day; cl 12 Nov until 3 Dec; (04 68 25 52 33. Remembering our first fantastic cassoulet in Carcassonne many years ago (before we ever recommended restaurants or even took note of them), we wondered if our luck would hold. Naturally we gravitated to Place Marcou, with all the other tourists. *Everyone* has cassoulet on the menu … so it became a matter of surreptitiously eyeing what was served in various places (so easy to do when all the tables are outside). We settled on the oddly-named Bistro Fruit — a restaurant, pizzeria, crêperie, bar and ice cream parlour, with something for everyone. Both the onion soup and the cassoulet were excellent, but they put paid to trying — or recommending — anything else on the menu! Two asides: the next night we tried an out-of-the-way restaurant which was not 'touristic' (that scourge of Trip Advisor reviewers). It looked appealing but was appalling… Every time we recommend a place in the 'tourist zone', we just *know* that it will be damned on Trip Advisor, but Bistro Fruit suited *us* splendidly; fast, pleasant service, clean tables, delicious food.

Cirque de Navacelles
LA BAUME AURIOL €-€€
D130 above the Cirque, daily all day Mar-Nov; (04 67 44 78 75; www.aubergedelabaumeauriol. com (under construction). We always like to approach the Cirque de Navacelles from the south, and that means passing the large Baume Auriol building and pulling up to take in the breathtaking view. Recently stopping for lunch, we found it under new management, with very helpful staff who were willing to make us a full lunch after 2.30pm. The chalk-board menus feature local — usually organic — produce: dishes like salmon and trout from the Vis, local suckling pig and lamb, local goats cheeses. Our freshly roasted vegetables were especially delicious. The *menu* is currently 26 € for three courses, but of course you can eat à la carte or just take a break with a drink on the terrace. *And of course the view is stupendous.*

To break Car tour 8 we used to stay in **Navacelles** itself, at the simple **AUBERGE DE LA CASCADE** €, cl 1/11-1/4; (04 67 81 50 95; www.auberge-de-la-cascade.fr. We hear it's under new management. No matter: staying there is as close to paradise as it gets.

Duilhac-sous-Peyrepertuse
AUBERGE DU MOULIN €€

9 Rue de la Fontaine, Duilhac, cl Mon and Nov-Mar; (04 68 48 95 34. The most idyllic setting, especially on fine days when one can eat out on the terrace under the huge willow beside the gurgling stream. The *auberge* specialises in local meats like wild boar and lamb and griddled fish of the day. *Menus* at 18 € and 27 €, but of course one can eat à la carte for less (Pat only had one course of gambas and accompanying vegetables, because the portions are huge). The service is efficient and friendly; this is *the* place to have a meal during a trip to the Corbières!

Lagrasse
We're fond of three places here, all very close together on the main D3 (Blvd de la Promenade). The most northerly (and best) is the **HOSTELLERIE DES CORBIERES** €€ ((04 68 43 16 56, www.hostelleriecorbieres.com), open all year, lunch and dinner, with traditional but inventively prepared, subtly-flavoured dishes (try the pigs cheeks, not often seen on menus). **Weekday** *formule* at 15 €; menus at 25 € and 35 €. Run by a husband/wife team; very friendly service. Terrace at the back, overlooking vineyards. A short way further along, on the other side of the road, is the **CAFE DE LA PROMENADE** €, open all day for snacks, but meals only at lunchtime, cl Jan ((04 68 43 15 89), a tiny place with tables outside on the 'Prom'. This is the friendly local, with very good, inexpensive food (*formule* 12 €). Ample choice, from salads and pastas to cassoulet or steaks. Good *frites*. Despite being 'prefab', the ice cream sweets are very good too. Further south, at the junction of the D212 to Fabrezan, is **L'AFFENAGE** €€ ((04 68 43 16 59), a pretty place with

a terrace on the 'Prom'. Dinner service only in summer, out of season open *most days* for coffee, tea and lunch. Good salads, otherwise fairly standard menu — the usual steak and duck.

Nîmes
PAVILLON DE LA FONTAINE €-€€

Quai Georges Clemenceau, daily all year from 08.00-23.00; (04 66 64 09 93; le-pavillon-de-la-fontaine.pagesperso-orange.fr. An oasis of calm in the heart of the city, just beside the Clemenceau Canal and facing the Temple of Diana. Watch the fish and the ducks from the large outdoor seating area — enjoying the shady terrace on a hot day or basking in winter sun. There's a very wide range of dishes (see their website), from paninis and a beer or crêpes and tea to an exotic three-course champagne dinner. Salads are a speciality — duck breasts with mangoes, seafood, aubergine caviar, carpaccios. Omelettes, kebabs, plenty of fish and meat. *Menus* at 16 € and 23 €; Mon-Fri luncheon *formule* at just 10.50 €. If it's still on the menu, don't miss the 'café gourmand', served with a tasting platter of mini fruits, pastries and puddings.

Pont du Gard
If you visit in the 'season', *do* have a meal at the traditional **LES TERRASSES** €€, on the right bank (*rive droite*) of the Gardon, with a wonderful view to the aqueduct; open for lunch Apr-Sep, for dinner Jun-Aug; (04 66 63 91 37; www.pontdugard.fr/content/restaurant-les-terrasses. Both **set and à la carte menus**. Here again, for us the setting is more important than the food. There's also a snack bar on the right bank, **Le Bistrot**. But the best option, if you just want a light meal *all year round* is to stay on the *rive gauche*, where there are four choices: a **café** serving

La Petite Gare at Vers, just west of Walk 7

hot and cold drinks, pastries and ice creams; **Le Snack** (regional dishes and fresh produce like salads); a **crêperie** with waffles as well as sweet and savoury crêpes; and **Le Vieux Moulin** (drinks, sandwiches, ice creams). On the other hand, **LA PETITE GARE** €€, 435 route d'Uzès, Vers Pont du Gard, (04 66 03 40 67; www.lapetitegare.net, can be guaranteed to give you a memorable meal. Open *only* Mon-Fri for lunch and Thu and Fri evenings. There are five or six *formules* from 14 € to 28 €. It's set in the old railway station at Vers, just west of the co-op at the start of Walk 7. The detailed website (only in French) is full of information and photos. Our gaspacho with tomato sorbet was heavenly, as were the beef tartare and Thai red chicken curry. A surprising but inspired touch: many dishes come with an **accompanying ice cream** — like lamb tartare with mustard ice cream. We hope this restaurant, in its slightly out-of-the way location, survives and flourishes!

Rieussec (near)
AUBERGE DE STE-COLOMBE €€
Col de Ste-Colombe near Rieussec (9.5km south of St-Pons, off the D907), open daily lunch and dinner (ex Wed dinner) in peak season, otherwise cl Mon/Tue evenings and all day Wed; *menus* from 13-38 €; (04 67 97 16 45, www.qualite-herault.fr. What a find — a gorgeous old farmhouse dating from 1746, with a bright and airy dining room — stone walls and yellow, blue or rose-coloured stencilled tables. Family-run and with a **huge menu** (look also at their entry on the website above). The à la carte menu lists **6 entrées**, **5 mains** and about **12 superlative sweets**. *But* be aware that there is *much more* on offer: hidden

away on the **8 set-price menus**, you'll find, for example, seasonal wild mushroom dishes. All the meals are served with a colourful selection of seasonal vegetables — when we last visited: pumpkin purée, potatoes *au gratin,* grilled tomatoes, mange-tout, and runner beans. Everything was very fresh and beautifully sauced; as the website says, the best of Hérault's local produce. *An ideal place for a meal near Walk 26 or 29.*

Roussillon
LE BISTROT DE ROUSSILLON €€
Place de la Mairie, cl Sun/Mon from 01/10 to 01/04 and Nov, otherwise open all day every day; **menus** at 15 € (2 courses) and 22 €); (04 90 05 74 45. This has been one of our favourite places for decades — great food and a lovely 'panoramic' terrace overlooking the ochre quarries (or eat outside in the square shown on page 77 and people-watch). Inside it's very cosy on a rainy day, with bright Provençal-style tablecloths. The menu is neither large nor exceptionally interesting, but the cooking and service are excellent. **6 salad starters**; the usual **meats** —steak, pork and lamb, but also beef carpaccio and beef tartare; for **fish** only salmon and tuna; plenty of **sweets** and exceptionally good **sorbets**. Of course there is also the **dish of the day** — the best bet, always very tasty.

Rustrel
LA RINSOULETTE €
West of the parking area for the Colorado Provençal, open 10.30-16.00 Apr-Oct, cl Mon ex Jul/Aug. We were not expecting anything special after checking

the Colorado walk, but this *buvette* just north of the aqueduct takes some beating! It seems to be a one-young-woman show, and she can really put together an eye-catching and tasty salad or tart (best tomatoes we've had in decades). If you are just after a light meal, look no further!

St-Michel de Frigolet
LE TREILLE €€
At the abbey (follow signs for 'buvette' from the entrance gate); cl Jan and Sun dinner/Mon outside summer, otherwise open from 10.00-21.30; (04 32 60 68 70; www.hotel-abbaye-frigolet. com. We used to love this place, which then closed for a few years, so we were delighted to see that it had reopened under new management. It's a lovely setting: for fine weather there's an outdoor terrace; in winter a roaring fire. The *carte* is extensive, ambitious and varied (unusual entrées like 'baby octopus with fennel bulb and *confit* of lemons'). There's a *menu* at 17 € (entrée/main/coffee or main/dessert/coffee). To be fair, we visited on a bank holiday, without booking, and they were very busy. We just ordered tomato salads and drinks. We were so glad we hadn't ordered anything else. We hope our experience was a one-off.

St-Pons
BAR DU PALAIS €
30 Grande Rue (behind the cathedral), open all day every day, (04 67 97 00 45; *formule* at 11.50 € (2 courses) — on the day we visited this was an omelette with *cèpes* (!) followed by an entrecôte/frites. You pass this cheap and tasty brasserie/café/glacier at the end of Walk 26. Eat under planes and lime trees, watching the world go by, then admire the cathedral and the lovely Hôtel de Ville opposite. Lots of salads, omelettes, sand-

wiches. Not often seen on menus: barbecued chicken wings with salad — it made a lovely light lunch.
If you want a really special meal near St-Pons, see under Rieussec.

St-Rémy
BISTROT DECOUVERTE €€-€€€
19 Boulevard Victor Hugo, 12.00-14.30 and 19.00-22.00, cl Sun evening, all day Mon, and 15/2-15.3; (04 90 92 34 49, www.bistrotdecouverte.com. Of the 90 or so restaurants in St-Rémy, this one is centrally placed on Victor Hugo, a few steps from the tourist office. It's owned by a husband/wife team; he worked in England with both Raymond Blanc and Marco Pierre White. With such a pedigree, this is not an inexpensive restaurant, but the *formule* is good value. The good house white is from the nearby Valdition estate; you can buy some from the wine cellar downstairs (*take care on the steep steps*). The **weekday lunch** *formule* at 15.50 € includes the dish of the day + dessert of the day; the more expensive '**menu**' at 30 € offers three courses, with a choice from 3 entrées, 3 mains and any sweet). The à la carte menu features **6 entrées** (soup, salads, terrines, snails, smoked salmon, ham), **4 mains** (beef tartare, lobster risotto, young duck with orange and honey, sirloin steak in green pepper sauce), **cheeses** from St-Rémy, and **5 desserts** — plus **two dishes of the day** and **more suggestions from the black-board** (including line-caught fish of the day). *Super food.* Be sure to check out their good website; it lists their speciality dishes and wines.

If you are visiting St-Rémy *in summer,* it might be worth trying the **Taberna Romana** at **Glanum** (open for lunch from 1/4 to 30/9). An article in the local paper whetted our appetites: the owner had prepared one of her Roman meals for a New Year's gala at St-Rémy. She emphasised how the Romans loved sweet-sour dishes, mixing Asian spices like ginger and Provençal herbs in the same dish.

Tarn, Gorges du

You're spoilt for choice with hotels — it all depends on where you want to be during the day. Look at all three websites below; all these hotels have superb food, terraces and a wonderful atmosphere. Arguably, *the* place in the Gorges is the **CHATEAU DE LA CAZE** €€€, some 5km northeast of La Malène on the D907b (℄ 04 66 48 51 01, www.chateau delacaze.com). It's *imperative to book ahead*, as it's almost always full. Although we'd stayed there in the past, we're not good at booking ahead. Finding it full some years ago, we drove south to **La Malène** proper, and the **MANOIR DE MONTESQUIOU** €€-€€€ (℄ 04 66 48 51 12, www. manoir-montesquiou.com). Since it was 'off season', and the hotel was not full, we were lucky enough to stay in the Chambre du Seigneur (see website) for a good price. This hotel is ideally situated for Walks 20 and 21 — and for watching all the comings and goings on the river. So it was our base for a few years … until the Viaduc de Millau was built and we wanted to be 'on the spot' for photography. Where better than the **GRAND HOTEL DE LA MUSE** €€-€€€ at **Le Rozier**, just beside the Tarn (℄ 05 65 62 60 01, www.hotel-delamuse.fr)? Totally different in atmosphere from the other two, it's a beautifully built modern haven.

Trèbes

LE MOULIN DE TREBES €€

2 Rue du Moulin, open daily ex Jan/Feb; ℄ 04 68 78 97 57; www.lemoulindetrebes.com. Weekday **lunch** *formules* at 13.50 € (two courses) or 15.80 €, evening *menus* at 23 €, 27 €. A really idyllic place just beside the Canal du Midi, with outdoor terrace and bright bistro-style dining room (exposed stone, wooden tables, bentwood chairs). There is a reasonably large *carte*, with real choice, *but beware:* it's only available at dinner or for lunch on the weekends — so don't work up a lunchtime appetite for frogs' legs on a Tuesday! For lunch in the week there is *only* the *formule*, which (when we last visited) was based on a large buffet, followed by either steak or the dish of the day. The cooking is plain and 'honest' (try the excellent disc-shaped *frites*), and the sizeable portions make it very good value for money.

Uzès

L'ECRIN DES SAVEURS €-€€

3 Boulevard Charles Gide, open all day every day, ℄ 04 66 22 35 21. This is a place we always stop, just opposite the northern entrance to the huge free car park by the Tour Fenestrelle. The choice of both Provençal and Italian specialities is huge, and there are **menus** starting at 9.50 € for lunch (dish of the day and salad). It is the perfect restaurant for us, with simple meals like omelettes, pastas, large selection of pizzas, mussels and chips — *or* any Provençal speciality you can name. There are other menus at 18.50 € and 25.50 € but, having seen the size of the 9.50 € *moules frites* with salad, we cannot imagine eating our way through anything more. The food is delicious, the service exceptional (but be warned, it gets *very* busy!). Outdoor seating in fine weather (but there will be some traffic noise).

Index

Geographical names comprises the only entries in this Index; for all other entries, see Contents, page 3. A page number in *italics* indicates a map; a page number in **bold** a photograph. Both of these may be in addition to a text reference on the same page. Recommended restaurants are shown by the symbol ✖; market days by the symbol ⚖.